Life's Greatest Grace

Life's Greatest Grace:

WHY I BELONG TO THE CATHOLIC CHURCH

J. MICHAEL MILLER
C.S.B.

Our Sunday Visitor Publishing Division
Our Sunday Visitor, Inc.
Huntington, Indiana 46750

Scripture texts contained in this work are taken from the *New Revised Standard Version Bible With Apocrypha*, © 1989 by the Division of Christian Education of the National Council of the Churches of Christ in the United States of America, and used by permission of the copyright owner. If any copyrighted materials have been inadvertently used in this work without proper credit being given, please notify Our Sunday Visitor in writing so that future printings of this work may be corrected accordingly.

Copyright © 1993 by Our Sunday Visitor Publishing Division
Our Sunday Visitor, Inc.

All rights reserved. With the exception of short excerpts for critical reviews, no part of this book may be reproduced in any manner whatsoever without permission in writing from the publisher. Write:
Our Sunday Visitor Publishing Division
Our Sunday Visitor, Inc.
200 Noll Plaza
Huntington, Indiana 46750

International Standard Book Number: 0-87973-477-9
Library of Congress Catalog Card Number: 92-60314

Cover design by Monica Watts

PRINTED IN THE UNITED STATES OF AMERICA

477

TABLE OF CONTENTS

INTRODUCTION

RELIGIOUS ETIQUETTE IN PLURALISTIC AMERICA DEMANDS THAT WE refrain from asking people *why* they believe what they do. "Why do you belong to the Catholic Church?" is jarringly direct. If, like Walker Percy, you are a little reckless, you might brashly answer, "Because it is true." But since most of us are reluctant to engage in a full-scale debate, we dodge the question by referring our Catholicism to our parents, education, or feelings. Significant as these reasons might be, they miss the mark.

Converts often bring a refreshing directness in answering this vital question cradle Catholics frequently shy away from. Wick Allison, a convert from Methodism, tells us that inevitably every thinking Christian confronts the claim of the Catholic Church — that claim which is "as outrageous as it is unavoidable."[1] Our nature calls us to seek the truth. Ultimately that truth is found only in Jesus Christ, who is both "the way, and the truth, and the life" (John 14:6) and the head of the Church, "which is his body, the fullness of him who fills all in all" (Ephesians 1:23).

You can of course be Christian without being Catholic. And, with God's grace, you can be virtuous without either confessing Jesus as Lord or belonging to the Catholic Church.

Although closely related to the question "Why am I a Christian?" it is not the same as asking, "Why belong to the *Catholic* Church?" It is this latter question that I wish to address.

For many years I have been working with Rite of Christian Initiation of Adults (RCIA) groups. This book has grown out of my experience of accompanying these aspiring Catholics on their journey. In countless ways their honesty, questions, and fervor have been an inspiration to me. They have forced me to examine more carefully why belonging to the Catholic Church is such an awesome grace, vocation, and responsibility. Time and again they prod me into reexamining the most fundamental reasons for embracing the faith — what cradle Catholics so often take for granted.

Throughout the book, I will use the term "convert" to refer to anyone who has become a Catholic Christian as an adult. If such persons are not yet baptized, they are called "catechumens" before entry into the Church. If they are already baptized, they are properly called "candidates" for full communion into the Catholic Church. In the United States, most new Catholics are "candidates," not catechumens. Since established usage is hard to break, I will use everyday language and refer to individuals from both groups as "converts."

When early Christians formulated their belief in the Church, they labeled it "Catholic." In both the Apostles' Creed and the Nicene Creed, we profess our belief in the Catholic Church. By the fourth century this designation had acquired two principal meanings, both of which remain relevant. For the Church to be Catholic means that she extends to the ends of the earth, including all the diversity of "saints from every tribe and language and people and nation" (Revelation 5:9). To be Catholic also indicates that the Church teaches *all* the truth revealed for our salvation.

This twofold wholeness is found, I believe, only in the Catholic Church. Writing fifteen hundred years ago, St. Augustine expressed it well: "Whether they intend it or not, even heretics and schismatics, if they are talking not among themselves but to outsiders, can only refer to one Church as catholic; namely the Catholic Church."[2] The great theologian had no doubt that Christ's Church was clearly recognizable in the doctrines, life, and worship of her adherents.

In this work, I would like to share with the reader some reasons why I believe that belonging to the Catholic Church is life's greatest grace. It is both personal and selective. By no means am I attempting to write a catechism that gives a full presentation of Catholic doctrine.

For those seeking a general compendium of the Catholic faith, the new *Catechism of the Catholic Church* is an invaluable resource. Pope John Paul II affirmed that its publication "must certainly be counted among the major events of the Church's recent history."[3] This "symphony of the faith" provides a sure norm for discovering what the Catholic Church believes. In light of Vatican II, the catechism explains the Catholic faith as it is believed, celebrated, lived, and prayed by the Church. In order to encourage its use, I have included many references to the *Catechism of the Catholic Church* so that readers will search out its riches for themselves.

Not organized around the articles of the Creed or the Ten Commandments, the twelve chapters of this book present selected themes that provide, at least in part, "an accounting for the hope" that is in me (cf. 1 Peter 3:15). Some chapters deal with doctrine, others with life. Together they provide some reasons, touching both the mind and the heart, for belonging to the Catholic Church.

If this book encourages those who are attracted to the Church to take the final step of joining her family, if it stimulates those who are troubled to remain within the fold, or if it helps those raised in the faith to articulate why they are Catholics and cherish that life, then it will have achieved its purpose. My reasons for being Catholic — and loving it — will not be identical with yours. But I hope that my reflections will inspire you to draw up your own list of reasons for belonging to the Catholic Church.

Cradle Catholics and Converts

MOST OF US WHO ARE PRACTICING THE FAITH TODAY WERE BORN into Catholic families that dutifully had us baptized and so inscribed our names on the rolls of the Church. We received our spiritual rebirth from the Church and were Catholics before we knew it, before we even asked for it. Others made the decision for us. Even though we might never have faced the question "Why belong to the Catholic Church?" with the same urgency as those seeking entry into the Church, cradle Catholics too should periodically take stock and reaffirm their ecclesial commitment.

Born Catholic?

To belong to the Catholic Church because of family tradition is a good beginning. Behind the practice of infant baptism is not only our parents' choice but the call of God. Only he can bring us into his Church. In the strict sense, no one is simply born Catholic. Everyone becomes a Catholic by the grace of God. We belong to the Catholic Church because God has called us here: "You did not choose me but I chose you" (John 15:16).

Despite the fact that the practice of baptizing babies might seem to obscure the individual's freedom consciously to choose the Church, Catholic pastoral practice remains bound to this "rule of immemorial tradition."[1] As the sacrament through which we enter the Church, baptism for the forgiveness of sins is for both infants and adults. For infants it guarantees that right from the beginning we are recipients and beneficiaries of God's unfathomable generosity. His tender mercy enfolds us from the font.

Why do I belong to the Catholic Church? Since I was baptized without asking for it, I can lay no claim to making any decision. Infant baptism manifests God's initiative and the gratuitous love with which he constantly surrounds us. The mystery of belonging to the Church is "not that we loved God but that he loved us" (1 John 4:10). If anyone is ever tempted to think of baptism as his or her own doing, infant baptism is a forceful reminder to everyone that all salvation comes from God as his unmerited gift. St. Paul wrote: "What do you have that you did not receive? And if you received it, why do you boast as if it were not a gift?" (1 Corinthians 4:7).

This divine call makes it clear to me that I do not belong to the Catholic Church because of my intelligence, my virtue, or my good works, but only because God has chosen me. Anything that would suggest that the Catholic faith is some kind of reward for good behavior is wrong from the outset. St. Paul was well aware that God does not choose the world's best: "Consider your own call, brothers and sisters: not many of you were wise by human standards, not many were powerful, not many were of noble birth. But God chose what is foolish in the world to shame the wise; God chose what is weak in the world to shame the strong; God chose what is low and despised in the world, things that are not, to reduce to nothing things that are" (1 Corinthians 1:26-28). Nothing in God's choice can flatter my ego. Like all grace, coming into the body of Christ is a pure gift of God (cf. Ephesians 2:8).

What's the real reason why I belong to the Catholic Church? Because in his goodness God has called me. There is something humbling, as well as mysterious, about this call. James Hitchcock once said that "as recipients of this gift we are less like victors in a race than winners in a lottery."[2] To be invited into the Church through baptism is an inestimable privilege that God squanders where he wills.

Growing Up Catholic

Many people say they belong to the Catholic Church simply because they grew up Catholic. Often intensely attached to the cultural and religious expressions of their youth, they wear medals, hang rosaries in their cars, display crucifixes in their homes, and call priests "Father."

Among these cradle Catholics are many who still devoutly practice their faith. Indeed, they remain the backbone of the Church. Others, who have never formally left the Church, are called "nominal" or non-practicing Catholics. They do not strive to live by the Church's teachings or celebrate her sacraments. Yet they are a vast number at the gates who still, at least in some sense, continue to belong to the Catholic Church. In *The Desolate City*, Anne Roche Muggeridge comments on this situation: "Catholicism is not just a religion: it is a country of the heart and of the mind. No matter how resolutely they turn their backs on it, people born within it never quite shed their accents."[3]

Undoubtedly Catholicism still represents a great cultural force, as the recent events in eastern Europe have so clearly manifested. It is impossible to mention the collapse of communism in Poland without alluding to the influence of the Pope and of Our Lady of Czestochowa. We also speak of Hispanic popular religion or Irish Catholicism as having a social impact that extends beyond the believing community. In some cultures, being Catholic is as much an ethnic reality as a religious one. People belong to the Catholic Church because they can't imagine belonging to any other.

Far be it from me to denigrate the vital importance of this feeling at home in the Catholic Church. If medieval men and women could camp out in cathedrals, moderns have every right to remain attached to the religion of their parents and their parish. But a merely sentimental affection for the Catholic faith is still a far cry from living the faith with joy and vitality.

Cultural explanations for belonging to the Church are not therefore wholly satisfying. To have Catholic roots is good, but it's not enough to say we belong to the Catholic Church just because we were baptized and absorbed Catholic customs. Being Catholic is more than being American — or Polish, Irish, or Hispanic. It is more than a simple fact of life. At some point cradle Catholics must render an account for being a Catholic adult.

Belonging to the Catholic Church seeps into the very marrow of our being. To be Catholic qualifies the way we truly are. We think Catholic, we act Catholic, we even talk Catholic. I love the Catholic Church because she has formed me, made me who I am — although she sometimes frustrates, angers, or disappoints me. Catholicism is as much a part of me as my arms and my legs. I agree with John Deedy: "I could no more cut it away and feel the same person than I could lop off a limb and not be aware that something vital has been severed from my person."[4] Those who have embraced the faith as adults are a great help to cradle Catholics who struggle with articulating their experience. The rich experiences of converts to the faith suggest many reasons for belonging to the Church that lifelong Catholics can ponder with profit.

Making the Choice as an Adult

After many years as a southern Baptist, a convert friend of mine once remarked that she had entered the Catholic Church because "Catholics have more fun." I doubt whether she was confessing to me the most profound reason why she had come into full communion with the See of Peter. But she did raise a crucial question — one that we have to come back to time and time again: Why do I belong to the *Catholic* Church?

For cradle Catholics such as myself, adult converts to the Church are, for many reasons, to be envied. Despite the spiritual head start of infant baptism, converts remind old-timers that we must thank God for bringing us into the Church. No one's pilgrimage to the fullness of the kingdom is on automatic pilot.

Day by day we must ratify our commitment to Christ and the Church. Crucial as it is, baptism is not the end, but the beginning, of our life of faith.

Conversion as an Ecclesial Event

The initial stages of thinking about whether one should become a Catholic Christian involve prayer, study, and judgment. Both the individual seeker and the believing community are involved. Prospective Catholics must want to embrace as their own that living tradition of teaching, life, and worship the Church proposes as her treasure. For its part, the community must determine that those seeking association are serious in their quest.

From start to finish, coming into the Catholic Church is an ecclesial event. To become a Catholic is to be received into that fellowship described by the apostle John: "We declare to you what we have seen and heard so that you also may have fellowship with us; and truly our fellowship is with the Father and with his Son Jesus Christ" (1 John 1:3). This emphasis on communion — on entering into the community of the Church for fellowship with God — does away with all religious isolationism, of being a church to oneself. If at one time the slogan "You can have Christ, without the Church!" tempted the inquirer, it must now be put aside.

Most adults who come into full communion with the Catholic Church are already Christians who believe in God, the authority of Scripture, the mystery of Christ's saving death and resurrection, the golden rule. They do not think about becoming Catholic because they think it is only in the Catholic Church that they can be "good." They know well enough that they can be "good people" without being Catholic, though of course an individual might be an even better person if God is calling him or her into the Catholic Church.

In the ceremonies of accepting the unbaptized as catechumens and of welcoming the already baptized as candidates for full communion into the Catholic Church, the congregation thanks God for leading them "by various paths to oneness in faith."[5] Potential converts must be able to say they have discerned God's call to the Church. If unbaptized, they ask for "faith." If baptized, they ask for "a fuller sharing in the life of the Church." In both instances, those who approach the Church do so with their arms open, asking the community to embrace them as fellow believers.

Who Chooses Whom?

From the converts' point of view, it appears as if they have chosen the Church. They feel attracted, they make inquiries, they pray — and then, by their own free choice, they ask to join. Converts often think of their radical step as the conscious decision of a mature adult. This attitude, I would hold, is only partially true.

When the psalmist sings, "My soul thirsts . . . for the living God" (Psalm 42:2), he is articulating a person's deep-seated need for the Truth. For most converts, this profound inner longing coincides with external circumstances that raise the question about belonging to the Church. Some experience of want or need that can never be fully described provokes the searcher to satisfy this longing by taking the first, often very painful, steps to the door of the Catholic Church. Without what St. Augustine called a "restlessness of heart," there would be no conversion. Content with the status quo, the self-satisfied show no curiosity about the Church. Behind this agitation is not despair but the sense of being called, invited, addressed — even though the reason for, or meaning of, the experience is not immediately clear.

Sometimes the original reasons for being attracted to the Church are amusing. The southern Catholic writer Flannery O'Connor humorously described why her cousin's husband, a professor at Auburn University, had entered the Church. In her explanation of his conversion, she wrote: "We asked how he got interested and his answer was that the sermons were so horrible (when he had gone to Mass with his wife), he knew there must be something else there to make people come."[6] Not a very profound reason, but God can turn any situation — even the most ordinary — into an occasion for grace.

"Convert stories," such as those found in *The New Catholics*,[7] explain in many different ways why the individual was first attracted to Catholicism. Some met Catholics who impressed them by the witness of their lifestyle, their conviction of the truth, or the firmness of their principles. Many others speak of the moral and religious clarity that they discerned in Catholicism. Like those in the Gospel who "were astounded by his teaching, for he taught as one having authority" (Mark 1:22), they recognized in the Church's preaching the gentle yet uncompromising authority of Christ. In fact, this is the most frequent reason new Catholics mention for getting on the road to Rome. Closely coupled with this cause is the papal ministry as exercised by Pope John Paul II. Time and again converts remark that they are drawn to the Church by his zeal, preaching, and moral authority.

In addition to such human and external reasons, those seeking to belong to the Catholic Church must also recall that theirs is the story of a call, or vocation, to the Church. Every conversion story begins with God himself. In the depths of their heart, converts recognize God's call: "Come, follow me" (Matthew 19:21) — come into my Church. Unable to bring about their own conversion, they can only acknowledge how God is acting within them. "Conversion is not something we do for ourselves but which God does in us."[8] He alone summons into the Church those who are to become Catholic Christians.

When examined prayerfully, what seems to be a haphazard road leading to the Church can be discerned as having a clear direction. For those who believe in divine providence, there are, strictly speaking, no accidents. Even without being aware of it, those seeking God in the Catholic Church have been prepared. Think of the seemingly sudden call of St. Paul (cf. Acts 9:3-6). What appears to have been a bolt from the blue had undoubtedly been divinely orchestrated. Perhaps his own violent persecution of Christians who did not yield or his witness of St. Stephen's willing martyrdom was the remote preparation for Paul's sudden encounter with the risen Lord. Indeed, he later recognized that God had set him apart even before he was born and had called him through his grace (cf. Galatians 1:15). Less dramatically this model has been repeated again and again in the life of the Church.

When asked why he joined the Catholic Church, Father Richard Neuhaus commented that "for me, becoming a Catholic was simply, steadily and inexorably moving in that direction for thirty years as a Lutheran pastor." It was a continuum, fulfillment, and consummation.[9] Nor must converts ever repudiate an earlier religious tradition that nourished them. In their own way, they prepare for entry into the Church.

Those seeking to become Catholics must therefore ask themselves why they want to belong to the Catholic Church. Even though it is impossible to describe conversion in purely human terms — since faith is an unmerited divine gift — nonetheless converts can profitably reflect on the means that God has marshaled to bring them to the Church's doorstep. Converts are usually able to chronicle their conversion — the people, events, books, or arguments that led them to raise the crucial questions: "What if the claims of the Catholic Church are true? Should I 'look into' it?" New Catholics delight in tracing the hand of God that brought them to the Church. Few exercises are more spiritually helpful in appreciating God's call than that of exploring how he has used the circumstances and people of everyday life for his own designs.

Unworthy Motives

Although the divine call always remains mysterious, converts must candidly examine whether their conscious motives for belonging to the Church can pass honest scrutiny. Undeniably the Lord brings us to the Church's threshold in curious, not to say puzzling, ways. But once given the chance to discern sincerely, the decision to enter the Catholic Church must not be made for reasons an individual knows to be unworthy.

Frequently people end up on the Church's doorstep because their husband or wife, fiancé or friend, has brought them there. Helpful as others can be in bringing us to Christ — after all, Andrew brought his brother Peter to Jesus (cf. John 1:41) — it is still the Lord who does the calling. To satisfy a loved one's pleas, to please family or peers — these are unworthy reasons for entering the Catholic Church. The only "pressure" we should feel is that exercised by the one whose yoke is sweet and whose burden is light (cf. Matthew 11:30).

Nor should a person think seriously of becoming Catholic if driven by a desire for emotional healing. Conversion is not primarily a matter of hoping for improved psychological stability or mental health. In short, prospective converts should be wary about approaching the Church with a cost-benefit mindset: What's in it for me? Wonderful as the close community spirit of the local parish might be, the feeling of security, the healing of guilt — none of these is sufficient motivation for becoming, or remaining, Catholic.

"Lifers" can undoubtedly tell converts that they are not Catholic just because the Church makes them feel good. The emotional rewards are a kind of fallout from belonging to the Church, not the reason for belonging itself. God's will must provoke conversion — not any expected social, intellectual, or emotional benefit.

The mere fact that the Church has survived for nearly two thousand years, despite her tumultuous history, sometimes attracts the curiosity of non-Catholics. Some might be attracted by the splendor of her monuments, the beauty of her chant, or the profundity of her intellectual achievements. Others might be more impressed by her service to the downtrodden, her siding with the weak, her long list of martyrs. Although a good prod for drawing people to investigate the Church's life, the solidity of her institutional grandeur cannot provide a sufficient reason for becoming Catholic. Converts must beware of seeking an ideal Church that corresponds to their own ideas of what Christ's Church should be like. Those who associate themselves with the Church because she provides a vision they find aesthetically pleasing, intellectually rigorous, or socially involved, will inevitably be disappointed. Desiring entry into the Church for these reasons misses what is most crucial.

Surely the question to be asked is not whether the Catholic Church meets my expectations but whether I meet the expectations of the Church! To seek a Church made after my own image is not to embrace the wounded body of Christ.

For those readers who are prospective Catholics, ask yourselves a few simple questions: Why do you want to become Catholic? How has God led you on this path? Who — and what — has been most influential in your journey? What kind of chronicle of your conversion could you write? Do you have any unworthy motives or unrealistic and therefore false expectations regarding the Church? Honest answers to these questions will lead to your own inventory of reasons for belonging to the Catholic Church and help you appreciate the rest of this book.

Faith and the Truth

TO BE A CATHOLIC IS TO ADOPT A DISTINCTIVE WORLDVIEW, A PARticular vision of reality. It means *to think* in a certain way. St. Paul had no doubts that entry into the Church brought with it an original way of thinking: "You were taught to put away your former way of life, your old self, corrupt and deluded by its lusts, and to be renewed in the spirit of your minds, and to clothe yourselves with the new self, created according to the likeness of God in true righteousness and holiness" (Ephesians 4:22-24).

Questions about the truth of the faith cannot be dismissed as irrelevant. I am not suggesting that becoming a Catholic is like taking a class and then passing the exam. But it does involve a turnaround, a *metanoia*, a new way of thinking. From Augustine, to Thomas Merton, to Dorothy Day, seekers have spent a long time informing themselves and puzzling over Catholic doctrine before committing themselves to the Church. What is Catholic teaching on the Holy Trinity? Why pray to Mary? What does the Church profess about purgatory? Why is she dead set against contraception and abortion? To make a profession of faith in the Catholic Church is the act of a thinking person. The Church calls her adherents to intellectual conversion. "From this free and liberating act of faith," writes John Paul II, "there flows a new vision of the world, a new approach to our brethren, a new way of existing as a leaven in society."[1]

At the last supper Jesus revealed to his disciples that he was their friend, that they were servants no longer (cf. John 15:13-14). He continues to invite us into friendship, since he makes known to us what he has heard from the Father (cf. John 15:15). In what does our friendship with Jesus consist? He draws us "into his confidence, and the sphere of confidence is the truth."[2]

To those whom he calls, the Lord gives a share in his own divine self-knowledge.

Submission to the divine truth is different from feeling comfortable with what the Church teaches. Her doctrine is hard to understand. Her moral teaching is tough to live by. When Jesus taught with spellbinding authority, he made many of his listeners uneasy. Though they complained that his teaching was difficult, he did not modify his message to prevent their being offended. He left them free and, as a result, the Gospel records that "many of his disciples turned back and no longer went about with him" (John 6:66).

In a matter as significant as religion, we cannot simply trust our feelings to guide us. For fallen humanity, feelings are *not* automatically to be trusted but rather to be mistrusted. Christopher Derrick warns: "My feelings are the fruit of my psychology, my childhood and education, my cultural conditioning: the state of my glands or my digestion can change them radically from one day to another. I wouldn't risk a penny on anything they told me. Yet all these people talk as though faith had no other basis and was therefore a blind and irrational thing."[3]

Don't bet your life, your eternal life, on how you feel about the Church. Belonging to the Church requires reasons, not feelings.

Faith and Reason

The Church, with her love of reason, rejoices in the truth wherever it can be found. St. Paul tells us: "Whatever is true, whatever is honorable, whatever is just, whatever is pure, whatever is pleasing, whatever is commendable, if there is any excellence and if there is anything worthy of praise, think about these things" (Philippians 4:8).

This complementarity of faith and reason came home to me recently when I was standing in the Stanza of Raphael, one of his beautifully frescoed rooms in the Vatican Museum. It vividly conveys something essential about why I belong to the Catholic Church. On opposite walls of this magnificent chamber painted for the papal palace are two sixteenth-century frescoes. The "School of Athens," with Plato and Aristotle surrounded by the great pagan philosophers, faces a fresco portraying the "Triumph of the Church," with the apostles and Fathers and Doctors of the Church adoring the mystery of the Holy Eucharist. Standing between them, one can take in at a single glance the profoundly Catholic vision that expresses our delight in the truth whether reached by reason or revelation. Catholics do not flee from the truth discovered by nonbelievers. Did not St. Augustine and St. Thomas Aquinas both draw immense wisdom from the writings of pagan Greek philosophers?

Many non-Catholics think that in matters of faith reason should be banished. We should not raise questions, they say, or seek reasons when faced with divine revelation. The great Protestant theologian Karl Barth was particularly vehement in his opposing reason as a "handmaiden" to faith. He delighted in maintaining that "I believe *because* it is absurd." For him, reason provides no support in coming to faith: "What could be more irrational and laughable, ridiculous and impossible, than God's words to Abraham? . . . Moreover, all the articles of our Christian belief are, when considered rationally, just as impossible and mendacious and preposterous. Faith, however, is completely abreast of the situation. It grips reason by the throat and strangles the beast."[4]

If God were to ask us to make an "irrational act," as Barth suggests, he would be calling into question the human nature he has made by failing to respect the order of creation. We are not holier, more godlike, if we forsake reason. Blind, uninformed faith is an affront to God by the person created "in his image" and likeness (cf. Genesis 1:27). Catholics do not surrender their reason by believing but go beyond it.

The scriptural images for faith are not blindness and darkness but vision and enlightenment. To believe is to embrace Christ, "the light of the world," and whoever follows him "will never walk in darkness but will have the light of life" (John 8:12). As God's gift, faith makes the person subject to his power so that natural reason is transcended. When God gives this gift, he does not do violence to the intellect but ennobles it with a new light. Faith is not a leap in the dark but a leap through the dark into the light. Faith is a risk; however, it does not consist of throwing ourselves into an unknown void but into arms that are ready to enfold us.

The Church expects believers to use their heads in believing. Though divine revelation exceeds the capacity of human reason to comprehend it, faith does not contradict reason. When enlightened by the gift of faith, reason can penetrate, although only partially, the truths that God has mercifully revealed to us. Choosing to become or remain a Catholic therefore involves your mind.

Almost with desperation, prospective converts often ask whether they have to *understand* everything the Church teaches before becoming Catholic. Do we first understand and then believe — or do we believe and then understand? Without undue subtlety, I would like to make two affirmations. First, reason leads a person to investigate the Church and to make a preliminary judgment about the "sensibleness" of Catholic teaching. Faith comes after this as a gift. Second, a venerable Church tradition insists that we must believe *so as to* understand. In his commentary on St. John's statement "But among you there are some who do not believe" (6:64), St. Augustine notes: "They do not understand *because* they do not believe. . . . We have believed *in order that* we might know; for, if we wished first to know and then to believe we would be able neither to know nor to believe."[5]

An example from interpersonal relations sheds some light on why it makes sense to hold that belief precedes understanding.

When they exchange vows, the bride and groom commit themselves to each other for life even though they have — by no means! — anything like total knowledge of the other. Each one accepts the risk of the unknown and entrusts his or her future to the other. Each has faith in the other. In the same way, we "believe" or commit ourselves to God before we really grasp very much about his love. That understanding comes very gradually and opens to eternal life when "we will see him as he is" (1 John 3:2) — "face to face" (1 Corinthians 13:12).

Trusting the Revealer

Catholic theology distinguishes two meanings of faith. At the same time it inseparably entails the heart's personal commitment to God and the mind's acceptance of what he has revealed to us.[6]

In everyday life, to say "I believe you" is to entrust yourself to or rely on someone. Here faith is less linked to some possible fact than to a person of whose trustworthiness you are certain. It always entails a relationship between persons and stands or falls with the reliability of the person who is believed.[7] Not unsure knowledge, faith is a "deep certainty founded on personal trust."[8] Abandoning self-reliance, a believer reaches out in trust to the other.

In a religious sense, when Catholics say they believe, they are attesting that God is the person in whom they trust — and in his Son, Jesus Christ: "Believe in God, believe also in me" (John 14:1). Having faith in God is having confidence in him. This is the trust of Abraham, who is recalled in the Eucharist as "our father in faith." He "obeyed when he was called to set out for a place he was to receive as an inheritance; and he set out, not knowing where he was going" (Hebrews 11:8).[9] The patriarch's response to the divine call tells us that faith is letting go of human security, self-abandonment to God's promise, an obedient decision to turn away from oneself by trusting in the Other.[10]

This is also Mary's faith at the annunciation when she

received her call to enter freely into God's saving plan. Holding back nothing of her own to rely on, she uttered her consent by responding, "Let it be with me according to your word" (Luke 1:38). She simply trusted in God — a trust that her cousin Elizabeth extolled at the visitation when she greeted Mary: "And blessed is she who believed that there would be a fulfillment of what was spoken to her by the Lord" (Luke 1:45).

Accepting the Message

For Catholics "faith" has yet another and equally important meaning. The Irish farewell greeting "Keep the faith" captures this idea succinctly. Here "the faith" is the message conveyed by the one trusted. When we say to a friend, "I believe in you," that declaration necessarily includes "I believe what you say." Faith in the person is verified by believing the message.

Similarly, trusting in God means that we accept his message as true. In the New Testament, faith refers to both the act of trusting in God and accepting the message revealed — the joyful proclamation that "Christ died for our sins in accordance with the scriptures, and that he was buried, and that he was raised on the third day in accordance with the scriptures" (1 Corinthians 15:3-4). It matters therefore not only *that* you believe but also *what* you believe.

The act of faith proceeds from our whole spiritual dynamic — from our intellect and will. It includes therefore embracing as true the Gospel handed down in the Church. According to the Letter to the Hebrews, "faith is the assurance of things hoped for, the conviction of things not seen" (11:1). Consequently, the believer's act of faith is total. Conditional surrender to God, faith with reservations, is self-contradictory. To have faith in God is to believe *all* that he has revealed.

Those who claim to believe in Jesus Christ but dismiss some of his teachings as outdated do not have faith in him. It is inconsistent to sever the messenger from the message. Jesus cannot be separated from his Gospel. Belonging to the Catholic Church therefore involves accepting *what* God has disclosed.

The Gospel deserves to be believed because God, who can neither deceive nor be deceived, attests to it.[11] Believers accept it precisely *as* God's word (cf. 2 Thessalonians 2:13). Because God cannot speak falsely, his word alone is a sufficient guarantee. A person with faith can say quite simply: "*God* has spoken; therefore I believe." Though we cannot provide arguments that win over skeptics, we ought not to be ashamed of admitting that our faith is sure. This certainty rests on the trustworthiness of God, not on mathematical proofs or deductive reasoning.[12]

In Christ, who is both truly God and truly man, God reveals himself. Christian faith rests on the divine-human words and actions of God's incarnate Son, "who is close to the Father's heart" and "has made him known" (John 1:18) — a revelation transmitted through the apostles in the Church. This message is authorized by God himself. Therefore: to believe Christ = to believe God. We submit freely to the Word heard because God guarantees this truth.[13]

Those who do not have faith often tell us that they wished they believed. Recognizing the fruits of belief, they yearn for its security and the meaning it gives to people's lives. Although we must admit that some do not believe, since they "loved darkness rather than light because their deeds were evil" (John 3:19), others — from all we can judge — have not received this precious gift. That is why we can never pressure or force conversion to the Church. God's ways are inscrutable (cf. Romans 11:33) and he gives the gift of faith to those whom he calls by prompting their will and enlightening their intellect.[14]

We come to faith only through his Spirit who moves the heart and opens the eyes of the mind to accept and believe the truth.[15] The call to the Church is neither the inevitable reward for good behavior nor the result of our own effort. Never a human right, it is a gift of God's grace (cf. John 6:44).

Catholicism and Objective Truth

Many people today are incensed at the very idea that the Church claims to teach with the authority of Christ, that listening to her word is the same as hearing his voice: "Whoever listens to you listens to me, and whoever rejects you rejects me" (Luke 10:16). In his devastating critique of American higher education, Allan Bloom, himself not a religious believer, recounted the incredulity of today's students when they are confronted with any claim to possess *the* truth. He tells us, "There is one thing a professor can be absolutely certain of: almost every student entering university believes, or says he believes, that truth is relative. If this belief is put to the test, one can count on the students' reaction: they will be uncomprehending."[16] Today's cultural climate makes people suspicious, if not hostile, to any claim at knowing truth. Indeed, they no longer regard truth as an objective datum but as a personal viewpoint without reference to reality. Truth becomes opinion, where everyone's view is equal.

The Catholic Church asserts her ability to distinguish truth from falsehood. Such truth is "universal, the same for all, which all can and must seek."[17] It is found ultimately in God who is Absolute Truth and in his Son, who identified himself with the Truth (cf. John 14:6). Such truth makes a claim not only on the mind but on the heart. It is lovable because it is discoverable in the person of Jesus.

The world considers anyone who claims to know the truth to be intolerant and dogmatic. Truth scares people because it upsets the popularly nurtured wisdom that we are all only its seekers. God forbid that anyone should claim to have found it!

The good news that we can know objective truth and an absolute right and wrong is not widely accepted. Moral and religious questions are systematically dealt with as individual matters with no foundation in "fact" but only in opinion. Peter Kreeft aptly notes: "The most pervasive mistake the modern world makes about faith is to subjectivize and psychologize it, as if believers constructed their religion out of their own psyches: 'I'm feeling rather religious today; do you have anything for me to believe in?' The mistake occurs because the modern mind has it inside out. It starts with the human rather than the divine. Thus its values are 'my values' (don't impose them on anyone else please!), and even truth is 'truth for me.' "[18]

Belonging to the Catholic Church commits you to accepting that God's truth in matters of faith and morals can be discerned. Catholics rejoice that God has revealed his saving truth in the Church. Never a cause for intolerance or arrogance, this truth is a treasure given to us so that by knowing it we may love it. You cannot claim to be Catholic and treat the Church as a debating society where truth is only elusive and everything is up for grabs.

Fullness of Truth

According to sociologists, the baby boomers are now returning to religion. Rejecting the senseless pursuit of wealth and success, this lost generation is now searching for religious experience. As heartening as this is in many ways, their quest is not necessarily the same as the pursuit of religious truth. Experts in the free market, they all too often select their religious beliefs and practices according to taste. As John Paul II has deplored, "They are subjectively attached to what pleases them, to what corresponds to their own experience, and to what does not impinge on their own habits."[19]

Swayed by this freedom of consumer choice, traditional religious denominations have changed their teachings and new ones have multiplied. Some churches are now made-to-measure according to the dictates of the customer. When these returning churchgoers look inside themselves for the answers — as society constantly invites them to do — they come up with a bewildering array of positions, doctrines, and practices. Not surprisingly, to put some order into this doctrinal chaos they construct their own "personal" religion, even if they associate themselves with a mainline community, including the Catholic Church.

A good argument can be made that this desire to choose which truths to believe is just the American way applied to religion. The fact that we did not lend a hand in writing the Gospel makes us wary of traditional orthodoxy. When religious individualism is rampant, people claim the right to decide for themselves what they like and dislike in any proposed teaching.

This attitude has also infiltrated the Catholic Church. As a result, many try to identify only partially with the Church, ignoring those truths they find unacceptable for one reason or another. Neither for cradle Catholics nor for prospective converts, however, is such an attitude defensible. On the contrary, belonging to the Catholic Church frees one from the imperialism of this senseless religious relativism.

Why is such picking and choosing among the Church's official teaching not authentic Catholicism? Personal selectivity of beliefs distorts the act of faith by divorcing it from the community. Despite the stirrings within some quarters that you can believe what you like and still be a "good practicing Catholic," such a notion compromises what true belonging means.

But isn't everyone entitled to believe what he or she wants? To this question Christopher Derrick wisely replies that before God and one's conscience, an individual is "absolutely obliged to conform his mind to apprehend reality, to face the facts, to live mentally in the real world." Then he adds, "To believe 'what you like' is to let your thought be governed by preference: it has sometimes been called 'wishful thinking,' and it is a prime sin of the intellect."[20] We are created to submit to truth, not to whim.

Compare adhering to the fullness of Church teaching to

loving another person. When you love someone unconditionally, the only love worthy of another person, you accept the other in his or her totality. You cannot love just the body or the brain and claim to love the person. Such dissecting is inevitably doomed to failure because it makes a fundamental error. We are to love whole persons, not just their pleasing characteristics.

In the same way, we are called to embrace the Church's faith. As the bride of Christ, the Church professes her faith in "one Lord, one faith, one baptism" (Ephesians 4:5). She is obliged to maintain her virginity, that is, the purity of her faith. All who approach her with love must embrace that wholeness. To belong to or possess her without welcoming that fullness of faith would be akin to defiling the Church. Being Catholic means espousing the integrity of revealed truth and omitting nothing.

Think how illogical it is for someone to say, "I believe *nearly* everything the Church teaches." What does this mean? Could such individuals really mean that they agree with the Church, unless they disagree with it — perhaps with its teaching on contraception, papal infallibility, or the divinity of Christ? Yet a good Catholic could say the same about Islam: "I agree with it" (about the existence of God, for example) "unless I disagree with it" (about the Trinity or the incarnation). But would you call yourself a Muslim because you agree with some, perhaps even many, of its principal religious teachings? Common sense and honesty tell us that by freely belonging to the Catholic Church we ought to profess what she proposes as her faith, not what we think it should be!

We receive our faith from the Church — not from pollsters, newscasters, theologians, or even individual priests. We are not baptized into our own faith but into the faith of the Church. It does not belong to isolated individuals but to the whole Church from the apostles down to Catholics of our own day. The Church offers her faith in its entirety to each generation. As a community of believers, her faith is normative for all who want to join her ranks.

Through the centuries many have attempted to discard official Church teachings. These "heretics" have chosen what they wanted to believe. That's what the Greek word "heretic" means: to select. A heretic simplifies the profound richness of the Church's wonderful story of God's merciful love for his creation. Let me give an example. In the fourth century, Arius, a pious monk from Alexandria in Egypt, denied the divinity of Christ. Why? Because he wanted to protect God's absolute transcendence. For him, the true God could not really have been born in a stable and suffered a criminal's crucifixion. He took a truth — God's transcendence — but tried to understand it using reason alone. In his theology, Arius ignored what the Church had taught and lived as essential in all thinking about the mystery of God: his Son's stupendous and redemptive incarnation. Arius tried to understand God one-sidedly, without taking into sufficient account *all* that God had revealed. By neglecting the fullness for the partial he ended up outside the Catholic Church — a heretic.

If you want to belong to the Church, you cannot select what you want and then put the rest aside as false or unimportant. Any tailor-made religion is fundamentally flawed. We do not try on the Church's teachings and then adjust them to make them fit. They come already made! Moreover, it is impossible to identify oneself totally with Christ and only partially with the Church. Nothing is partial in Jesus or the Church he founded. You cannot have Christ in word and sacrament apart from his body, the Church. As "one flesh" (cf. Ephesians 5:21-32), what God has joined no one can put asunder. To be a Catholic is to believe all that the Church solemnly teaches and believes. In the traditional Act of Faith, we pray: "O my God, I most firmly believe in you and *all* you have revealed to your holy Catholic Church."

Prospective Catholics must be ready to assent to all that the Church teaches. As a visible institution, she has visible limits.

To enter the Church as a dissenter would be dishonest. Hans Urs von Balthasar says: "If someone cannot identify himself with the apostolic faith of the Catholic Church, nobody hinders him from distancing himself from it. What advantage would he have from confessing this faith and at the same time falsifying it from himself and others?"[21] If a person is unable to make a full profession of faith, then he or she is not yet ready to be a Catholic.

At the beginning of one's journey to the Church, an inquirer might not yet agree with everything the Church teaches. But that should be expected! Catechumens and candidates need time to learn and reflect on Catholic doctrine. Before baptism or entry into full Church communion, one must certainly know and accept her core doctrines and believe that whatever she teaches with full authority is true. An honest Catholic cannot *reject* anything that he or she knows the Church solemnly teaches.

Admittedly there might still be doctrines whose meaning is obscure, even very obscure, or only of peripheral interest. One might, for example, not understand or care too much about indulgences. Paul Vitz, himself a convert, uses an analogy from marriage: "When you get married you certainly don't know or understand everything about your bride — God forbid! Instead, you are confident that as you get to know her over the years your love and allegiance will grow."[22] Ignorance of the truth and not understanding it is, in varying degrees, the lot of every Catholic. Entering the Church would be unprincipled only if one understood a point of Catholic doctrine and then denied it.

I belong to the Catholic Church because her vision of God and the world are firmly grounded in reality. Accepting her teachings does no violence to my mind. True faith, like true love, gives sight. The Church defends both the reasonableness of reality and the profound truth that ultimate meaning only comes through Jesus Christ. Against the rising tide of relativism and individualism she stands firm, humbly holding and passing on the good news of Jesus' death and resurrection. She knows and cares for what she teaches with the passion of an ardent lover. Grateful for the gift of faith, I am saved from succumbing to any project for a private Christianity by being embraced by the faith of the Church.

Built Upon the Foundation of the Apostles

IN THE FIRST EUCHARISTIC PRAYER OF THE MASS, THE ANCIENT Roman Canon, the celebrant prays for all pastors who "hold and teach the catholic faith that comes to us from the apostles." I belong to the Catholic Church because she bequeaths to me the apostolic faith — the faith of Peter and Paul, Andrew, James, John, and all of Jesus' other companions. Today Catholics in Houston, Calcutta, Budapest, or São Paolo all share the same true faith. Though its celebration in liturgy, theology, and piety might vary, everywhere it is the faith of the Church that at baptism we say we are proud to profess.

Those who want to know Christ and his authentic teachings, and not the innumerable substitutes and errors that have claimed his authority through the centuries, must be assured that what they believe is not twisted. How do we know that what we "hear" and "learn" in the Church is really the "Gospel truth" — the word of God from the Word of God himself? Fundamental to Catholicism is the conviction that the Church, like St. Paul, has passed on the apostolic faith without distortion (cf. 1 Corinthians 15:3).

The New Testament records that right at the beginning those who believed in Jesus shared "one faith" (Ephesians 4:5) and held fast to their founder's teachings. Jesus had himself chosen, trained, and commissioned its nucleus, the Twelve. As a community it knew that it was "entrusted with continuing his concerns and even his presence."[1] The first Christians did not believe what they wanted to but embraced the faith preached to them by the apostles and those whom they had commissioned to spread the good news. Down through time, all those who wish to join the community of the Church espouse this same apostolic faith.

Only if we remain in the "company of the saints" — the Church — can we "comprehend . . . what is the breadth and length and height and depth" (Ephesians 3:18) of knowing Christ Jesus. The witness of the Church is an essential element in revelation itself. Walter Kasper writes: "Only in and through the Church does the revelation in Christ reach its goal. Only in and through the Church does it attain persistence and efficacy in the world."[2] Although faith is always a personal attachment to Jesus, it also has a content that belongs primarily to the community of believers, the custodians of the original apostolic deposit. Consequently, without the Church, "no individual can assess for himself what constitutes Catholic reality."[3] Only by clinging to the Church can one enter her mystery.

Accessing the Origins of Truth

How we "access" that public faith of the Christian community is therefore critical. Is it through Scripture? It certainly is. The Catholic Church is the Church of the Scriptures. Is it *only* through sacred Scripture? No, it is not.

God has not just spoken to his people through his representatives, the prophets, but in the fullness of time he has spoken through his Son (cf. Hebrews 1:1-2). "No one has ever seen God. It is God the only Son, who is close to the Father's heart, who has made him known" (John 1:18). How has the Son made God known? By speaking to us directly in the actions and words of Jesus, the Word made flesh (cf. John 1:14). The Son of God is the Word of the Father who was "in the beginning" (John 1:1). When he assumed human nature, his words and actions were therefore truly divine: "He whom God has sent speaks the words of God" (John 3:34). Jesus gave his followers more than a word about God or from God. In him, the very Word of God addressed humanity. Until the risen Lord comes again in glory, no further revelation will take place that will tell us more about God than what has already occurred in Jesus' life, death, and resurrection.[4] Through the centuries, the Church's study, contemplation, and teaching scrutinize ever more deeply the meaning of this once-and-for-all revelation.[5]

Jesus himself was not only the way and the life but also the truth (cf. John 14:6) in person. He spent his public ministry as a teacher, preparing the Twelve for their mission. As the eternal Son of the Father, Jesus is the definitive Teacher who said that "the word that you hear is not mine, but is from the Father who sent me" (John 14:24). In his entire being, through action and word, and especially through his death, resurrection, and sending the Spirit of Truth, Christ is himself the fullness of grace and truth (cf. John 1:14).

Since God has disclosed himself to humanity in a way that has reached its culmination in Jesus Christ, it is crucial that this definitive divine revelation should reach us uncorrupted. Only if this is true can we know that we are encountering the word of God and not human opinions. At the end of the twentieth century, how do Americans find this original revelation first delivered to the apostles?

Sharing in Christ's power, the apostles were authoritative witnesses to him and the foundation stones of his Church (cf. Ephesians 2:20). Not volunteers, the Twelve were called into service. During Jesus' public ministry they did not understand fully who he really was or what their own role was to be in his kingdom. After his death and resurrection, however, they reflected on their firsthand experience and began to grasp the Master's teaching and the astonishing events of his life. Having experienced him risen bodily from the dead, they were prepared for the pentecostal impact of the Spirit. Without this Pentecost gift, the apostles would have been unable to understand who Jesus was and what he had done for the world.

The apostles could take up their task of preaching the good

news because the Holy Spirit equipped them for it. If they had relied on a merely human authority they could not have guaranteed for us the reliability of their witness. "By sending the Holy Spirit, Jesus Christ confirmed with divine testimony what Revelation proclaimed."[6] Because of their transformation at Pentecost, the apostles had the assistance of a new light that illumined what they had seen and heard before Jesus' resurrection from the dead. The Holy Spirit revealed the Son to the apostles by bringing to light the *meaning* of the words and actions of his life (cf. John 16:13) so that they could preach the whole Gospel truth.

As Jesus spoke of the Father, not of himself, so did the Holy Spirit not speak of himself but of the Son. Because of this interior testimony, the apostles could understand God's designs in Christ, "a plan for the fullness of time, to gather up all things in him" (Ephesians 1:10), even before they clearly formulated their experience in words.

What we yearn for is the truth of Christ — not the erroneous opinions of well-intentioned but mistaken preachers. As a way of guaranteeing that Jesus' original teaching would remain uncorrupted so that all generations would receive divine revelation, "God graciously arranged that the things he had once revealed for the salvation of all peoples should remain in their entirety, throughout the ages, and be transmitted to all generations."[7] Catholics gratefully acknowledge that Christ's word of truth abides in the Church's deposit of faith (cf. 1 Timothy 6:20; 2 Timothy 1:14). If it did not, then Jesus would not have kept his promise that the gates of hell would not prevail against it (cf. Matthew 16:19). The Church's unequivocal claim to speak for Christ would be presumptuous and evil if she had no divine pledge assuring that her Gospel would remain undefiled. Belonging to the Catholic Church gives one the surety of encountering "the real thing" — Jesus as he mercifully revealed himself to sinful humanity.

Passing on Apostolic Life and Teaching

Every religion that preserves a foundational experience for succeeding generations depends on tradition for its continued existence through time. Religious tradition is the handing on of a particular experience of God's intervention in the world. It is the instrument through which the original revelation is shared with those who were not firsthand eyewitnesses or participants.

The English word "tradition" translates the Greek word for "handing over." Everything we live and believe in the Catholic Church is received — even the Holy Spirit breathed into her to complete Christ's work on earth. "What do you have that you did not receive?" demanded Paul (1 Corinthians 4:7). "Nothing at all," we must answer.

To belong to the Catholic Church means to join a people that has laid hold of Christ's foundational teaching and life. It is in and through this ecclesial community that we receive the story of Jesus Christ, the revelation first given to the apostles. The Church is entrusted with safeguarding this tradition so that she can continue to bear witness to Christ. Catholics believe that the original apostolic preaching is preserved in the community led by its successors — the bishops. Right from her beginning, the Church has preserved the original revelation of Jesus in her life, teaching, and sacramental worship. To hand on Jesus' teaching and life, the Church uses the means that the Lord has given her: the Bible, creeds, worship, and the living authority of the bishops who are responsible for the safeguarding and continual transmission of the deposit of faith.[8]

The French theologian Yves Congar points out that "the economy [of salvation] begins by a divine transmission or tradition."[9] From the inner trinitarian life of God, to the incarnation, to the death of Jesus and the mystery of Pentecost, all is "handed over" from God for us and for our salvation. Writing at the end of the first century, St. Clement of Rome described this divinely orchestrated "handing over": "The apostles received the gospel for us from the Lord Jesus Christ . . . [who] was sent from God. Thus Christ is from God, the apostles from Christ: in both cases the process was orderly and derived from the will of God."[10]

In the broadest sense, sacred tradition is synonymous with such general terms as the "Gospel" or "revelation." It is the means by which the whole mystery of Christ — what he taught, how believers worshiped, and how they lived — is communicated to every generation.

St. Athanasius, a fourth-century Father of the Church, describes tradition as "what the Lord gave, the apostles proclaimed and the Fathers guarded."[11] What Christ "gave" was more than a series of truths to believe. He came so that we might "have life, and have it abundantly" (John 10:10). The Master not only taught the apostles, he invited them to imitate him. They "followed" him in all things. Similarly, the first Christian converts "devoted themselves to the apostles' teaching and fellowship, to the breaking of bread and the prayers" (Acts 2:42). After Pentecost the apostolic community lived "the tradition" even though it was not yet written down. With the passage of time, this tradition gradually came to be *explicitly* expressed.

Sacred tradition therefore communicates the entire apostolic heritage: what is written and unwritten — the Church's teaching, practices, liturgy, institutions, and moral principles. The Vatican II Council Fathers defined sacred tradition as follows: "Now what was handed on by the apostles includes everything that contributes toward the holiness of life and increase of faith of the People of God; and so the Church, in her teaching, life, and worship, perpetuates and hands on to all generations all that she herself is, all that she believes."[12]

Their description includes Scripture as an essential element of the sacred tradition that nourishes the Church's life.

Nonetheless, the transmission of the Church's faith did not depend on writing it down. When tradition is broadly understood, it includes the Scriptures. In the mid-second century, St. Irenaeus of Lyons made this point clearly: "If the apostles themselves had left us no scripture, would it not be necessary to follow the 'order of tradition' that they have transmitted to those to whom they entrusted the churches?"[13] Tradition, then, precedes the New Testament in its witness to Christ.

How do we know that sacred tradition is a reliable witness to the original Gospel? Because of the Spirit's presence, the authenticity of the apostolic preaching is preserved in the Catholic Church.

Written Tradition: The New Testament

Beginning with Pentecost, the apostles and their associates expressed in their preaching, worship, and manner of life what they had experienced with the Lord. This "Way" (cf. Acts 9:2) is what they proclaimed to others. Jesus had given them no primer or teacher's manual. Yet already during the lifetime of the first generation of believers, some of this apostolic tradition was written down in those books we now call the New Testament. Undoubtedly these writings tell us the definitive truth of divine revelation.[14] Though they are "the principal witness for the life and teaching of the incarnate Word, our Savior,"[15] they make no claim to record *everything* in the original apostolic preaching and life. Nevertheless, together with tradition, the New Testament is now indispensable to the Church's life.

The apostles' preaching and writing were not like those of an observer who might have seen or written down the events of Christ's life from a journalistic perspective. When the sacred authors recorded in writing their life with Christ, the Spirit inspired them so that they would not mislead others. Having guarded their preaching from error, the Holy Spirit also assisted them in their writings so that what they wrote down was what God wanted.[16]

The Catholic Church is both the proprietor of Scripture and

its obedient servant. It was only because of her authoritative selection that the various books claiming to bear witness to the apostolic preaching were sorted out and designated as authentic. This "canonization" of Scripture was the work of the Spirit who guided the bishops of the Church.[17] The New Testament is the product of the believing community's process of handing over her life and teaching. If it weren't for the Catholic Church we wouldn't have any New Testament! The truth of Jesus Christ is presented and communicated in a human way — through the Church's proclamation, life, and activity.[18]

Since the Church articulated her faith and life in the sacred writings, she remains the only instrument competent to interpret them. Because the Church knows what she believes, she can therefore assert what the Scriptures mean.[19] Submissive to what God has revealed, she safeguards this revelation for us.

The Fathers at Vatican II recognized that "sacred tradition and sacred scripture form one sacred deposit of the Word of God, committed to the Church."[20] Both come from the same divine source and both have as their purpose communicating revelation, the mystery of Christ, to all generations. Together they testify to God's saving work on our behalf. Scripture and tradition together make up the one apostolic heritage, the deposit of faith, which the Church is faithfully to preserve (cf. 1 Timothy 6:10; 2 Timothy 1:14).

Although the "cart" is Scripture, the "horse" is the Church. Sacred tradition includes Scripture. From the beginning, the New Testament was transmitted along with sacred tradition, since not everything Christians believed or lived was written down. Nor could it have been. When the community "passed on" its sacred writings, it did so necessarily *within sacred tradition*. The key to the Scriptures must be received from the Church's tradition of the Church, as from the Lord himself.[21] Therefore, Scripture can only be understood in light of the tradition that formed it and the Church that now "lives" it. The

Gospel was not handed down to the community in lifeless documents; it is written in the hearts of believers by the Holy Spirit (cf. 2 Corinthians 3:3). At the same time, the Church is herself forever ruled by Scripture.

All of us are beneficiaries of the Church's great "handing on," or tradition. Without holy Church we would have no Scriptures, no sacraments, and no guidance on how to live as Christians.

Living Tradition

Despite popular opinion, the Church's tradition is not stagnant. It is ever living and vital, building upon "the foundation laid by our fathers in the faith, and particularly upon what the 'Apostles passed down to the Church' in the name of Jesus Christ, who is her irreplaceable foundation (cf. I Corinthians 3:11)."[22] Like the householder "who brings out of his treasure what is new and what is old" (Matthew 13:52), the Church's tradition develops with the people of God on pilgrimage.

The French writer Paul Claudel compared the Church's tradition to walking, with one foot on the ground and the other in the air. Tradition has an enduring element — it is rooted in the apostolic preaching, and an openness to change — moving forward through time under the guidance of the Spirit. Since it looks back to its undisputed point of reference in Jesus Christ, sacred tradition is essentially conservative. Never needing essential reconstruction, since "Jesus Christ is the same yesterday and today and forever" (Hebrews 13:8), the great tradition is also open to the future. If we keep both feet on the ground, we do not budge, becoming intransigent or reactionary. If we have both feet in the air, we are foolhardy and lose our bearing.

Sacred tradition can therefore be described as a progressive conservatism. It provides us with a framework for permanence and a means through which authentic development can take place. This rich tradition must be passed on from generation to generation. As it is handed on, tradition "progresses in the Church, with the assistance of the Holy Spirit. . . . Thus, as the centuries go by, the Church is always advancing towards the plenitude of divine truth."[23] This dynamic character of sacred tradition, though permanently linked to the apostolic heritage, means that Church teaching develops through time. Avery Dulles points out that Catholics can "cheerfully admit that some of their dogmas would have been unknown and even unintelligible to Christians of the early centuries."[24] A "new" dogma, like the Immaculate Conception, enters into sacred tradition insofar as it is guided by the Spirit, who empowers the Church to discern the truth.

Though the Pope and bishops have an irreplaceable role in safeguarding its integrity, tradition is transmitted primarily by laypeople who witness to this faith by their lives at home, work, and in the community. Undeniably, schools, religious education programs, parishes, and especially Sunday Mass, play their role in "traditioning" the faith. But it is primarily the family, the "domestic Church," that bears this responsibility. In the home, the young are taught, by word and example, what it means to be Catholic.

Catholic Traditions

The Catholic reverence for sacred tradition should not, however, be confused with "traditionalism," the cult of the outdated for its own sake. Loving the tradition is not a fondness for archaic language, quaint dress, Gothic churches, and Latin hymns. Catholics worship the Lord who "is making all things new" (cf. Revelation 21:5) and are not old-fashioned in this sense. Belonging to the Catholic Church is not like having membership in a stodgy men's club.

Yet Catholics rightfully cherish "small t" traditions. Not to be equated with sacred tradition, such Catholic customs — from the Advent wreath, to holy water, to blessed ashes and the rosary — keep us in touch with the Church as she has developed through the ages. Not essential to the faith, as that heritage coming from the apostles, these customs nonetheless help us to understand the mystery of the incarnation, the need for conversion, our belief in the communion of saints.[25] When such Church traditions are out of step with secular culture, they alert us to what is unique about religious belief. We do not, after all, genuflect anywhere except in church! Furthermore, traditions are necessary if what we pass on is to be alive, colorful, and imbued with the wonder of the Word made flesh. Just as Americans use the Stars and Stripes, the Pledge of Allegiance, and the Fourth of July to bind citizens together, so does the Church have its traditions. "Without its network of crucifixes, feast days, hymns, and professions of faith, Catholicism could scarcely maintain itself as an enduring worldwide society."[26] Traditions bind Catholics together not only across space but through time, linking us to our ancestors in the faith.

In its fundamental faith, today's Church is the same as that of the apostles, of St. Augustine, of the crusaders, of St. Teresa of Ávila, of John Carroll, of our grandparents. Our Catholic roots reach out across time and culture. We form part of a great family, a living stream. Each of us is involved in a community that goes far beyond any individual. The simplicity of Francis and the tough sweetness of the Little Flower belong to us. These are our people, our tradition. St. Peter's is as much ours as John Paul II's. The splendid tapestry of Catholic traditions is exuberant.

We cannot of course place the Church's human traditions on the same level as sacred tradition. Any particular tradition can fail to express the Gospel and even stifle needed renewal. Jesus' warning about abandoning the divine commandments and holding to human traditions (cf. Mark 7:1-13) is a salutary reminder of our need to scrutinize them. Human traditions *can* obscure the great apostolic tradition. Consequently, these traditions need constant purification and renewal.[27] Nevertheless, they play an invaluable role in the Church's life and culture.

It would impoverish Catholicism to denude it of its "culture" that is transmitted by this rich variety of traditions, whether they are pious practices, religious art, devotional folk customs, or ways of speaking. A people without traditions becomes rootless and deprived. Although debunking Catholic customs has become fashionable, these traditions can serve to highlight the central message of the Gospel.

I belong to the Catholic Church because I believe that here access to Jesus himself is assured — to his teaching and to the celebration of his saving death and resurrection. "We 'have' the reality and truth of Christ only through mediation of the Church's witness, which is sustained by the Holy Spirit. Without the Church, we 'have' no Christ, no Gospel and no Bible."[28] The Catholic faith comes to us from the apostles and is preserved, by God's mercy, in his Church. Through her life, confession, and celebration of divine worship, the Church bears witnesses to her faith before the world. She is truly the "pillar and bulwark of truth" (1 Timothy 3:15).

Teachers in the Church

ALL CHRISTIANS HOLD THAT THE GOSPEL IS THEIR STANDARD OF belief. Catholics are no exception. We are hearers of the word of God to which we must be submissive. But belonging to the Catholic Church also brings with it a heartfelt gratitude for a specific way in which Christ's teaching comes to us — through the successors of the apostles.

Though Catholics sometimes gripe about their bishops, teasing them for their pomposity, criticizing them for meddling in economic and political affairs, and chastising them for not being tough enough — or too tough — without these men the Church would cease to be Catholic. Among the principal reasons for belonging to the Catholic Church is her preservation of this apostolic ministry. In today's Church, the bishops carry out the teaching and pastoral office Jesus first gave to the Twelve.

Why We Need Teachers

Pope John XXIII entitled one of his encyclicals *Mater et Magistra* because the Church is *both* our mother and our teacher. As mother, she nourishes us with the grace of the sacraments. "Receiving life from the Spirit, she 'generates' sons and daughters of the human race to a new life in Christ."[1] As teacher, she helps us to have the "same mind . . . that was in Christ Jesus" (Philippians 2:5) and to fulfill "the law of Christ" (Galatians 6:2). Good mother that she is, the Church does more than offer vague doctrinal suggestions and moral encouragement and affirmation. The Church dares to teach the truth with authority!

Despite Americans' innate dislike of being told what to do, our schools, the leaders of opinion trumpeted by television, and the mass media are instructing us all the time, trying to cajole, persuade, and manipulate us. Let there be no mistake about it. The so-called "real world" of economic hardship, marital strife, and cruel competition — where the rules of the game are not those of the Gospel — has us as captive pupils. They are relentlessly teaching us about who we are, what we should be doing, and what the world should be like. No one doubts that we are being molded by Madison Avenue, sit-coms, and the solicited statements of stars and athletes. Even if these teachers do not pontificate on the mystery of the Trinity, they do so glibly on other questions of more than marginal concern to Catholics: what we think (and do!) about the big three — money, power, and sex. I, for one, am very grateful that the Church provides an alternative voice to the confusing chorus that is constantly shaping our religious and moral life.

If we are to believe the pollsters, then this pseudo-teaching has had its effect. We are constantly being barraged by statistics telling us bad news about our low levels of premarital chastity, high number of abortions, and increasing tolerance to same-sex unions. It doesn't take a genius to see the huge gap between what the Church is officially teaching and how people are living. Such surveys not only inform, they teach us. Their implicit message is always the same: "Go with the flow." One possible response would be for the Church to overlook the scriptural admonition about not being conformed to the spirit of this world (cf. Romans 12:2) and throw in the towel. By doing this the Church might, say the tempters, win more friends and gain more influence. The only acceptable alternative, however, is for the Church to go on proclaiming the Gospel with persistence — convincing, rebuking, and encouraging "whether the time is favorable or unfavorable" (2 Timothy 4:2). Fidelity to Christ demands this.

Without attempting a definitive list, I would like to mention a few of the principal "lessons" that society, especially through the mass media, is pounding into our heads. First is the cult of individualism that isolates the person from the community and makes him or her incapable of true human relationships. This inevitably leads to a loneliness that seeks substitutes in hedonism and the flight from responsibility. Leaving all your options open is praised, and life's highest goal is self-fulfillment. In religious matters, the spinoff is obvious. "An increasing number of Christians seem to have a reduced sensitivity to the universality and objectivity of the doctrine of the faith," writes the Pope, "because they are subjectively attached to what pleases them, to what corresponds to their own experience, and to what does not impinge on their own habits."[2] A second lesson being taught is that material well-being will bring happiness. An all-consuming passion for "having" leads people to seek a life of enjoyment. When people become slaves of their possessions and of immediate gratification, their thirst for God easily becomes stifled.[3] Consumerism, selfishness, and a willingness to exploit others to maintain one's level of pleasure become commonplace. A hedonistic society based on individualism, the cult of self-fulfillment, and materialism is constantly seeking recruits for its ranks, graduating ever more students who have learned its lessons.

How does this teaching take place? Let me suggest a simple scheme to you. A generation ago, societal and Church norms on many moral questions were mutually supportive. This was so, for example, in the area of sexual mores. Then, beginning in the 1950s and exploding in the '60s, came the sexual revolution. It was slow and timid when it began. The first move was made by singles. Premarital relations became more widespread before marriage, replacing the norm of limiting conjugal relations to the married. Soon living together was accepted as ordinary. Then premarital sex was recommended as the preferable preparation for marriage.

This "teaching" unfolded with relentless clarity: What had

once been condemned became tolerated, then normative, then a "right" questioned only by bigots. Who could deny that we have all been taught about sex from the world we live in? We all learn from society not only about how to live our sexuality but also about how to deal with unwanted pregnancies, about the morality of nuclear war, about the power of money.

For me, belonging to the Church means that I am challenged to accept an alternative to prevailing conventional wisdom in moral questions. Is it true, for example, that abortion is a "woman's right"? Are there any limits to genetic experimentation and manipulation? Is a policy that has civilians targeted in a retaliatory military attack morally acceptable? The Church makes no bones about claiming the right to form the conscience of her members. This flies in the face of secular opinion. At the core of secularization is the simple rule: Keep religion in its own separate compartment where it has no influence on the rest of life! The Church, however, insists on her own mandate, her obligation to form a vision, an outlook on the world, which is distinctly Catholic. Belonging to the Church is not like attending part-time classes that affect us peripherally. Her teaching impacts the nitty-gritty of life.

If the Church exists to foster our relation with Christ, then she must be able to teach us about the whole person who encounters him — and not just a narrow slice of our being from which are stripped our struggles with money, sex, and power. When the Church teaches, she does not make suggestions or merely enunciate ideals that no one can fulfill. Instead, across the centuries, she teaches us the way of Christ, a teaching that frequently contradicts the popular dogma of relativism.

Undoubtedly society's teaching role is less forceful in specific issues of faith and morals than in the spirit it gives us to breathe. I think honesty compels us to admit that this spirit is hostile to a religious authority that claims to offer more than a set of opinions. Insofar as Americans, even believers, are children of the age, they have imbibed this attitude and fallen prey to religious and moral relativism. When religion becomes a purely private matter, primarily one of feelings (which in conventional wisdom cannot be challenged), then accepting teachers with real authority does not come naturally.

Given this American spirit where people are supposed to maximize their own independence or freedom, many fail to see the need for teaching authority in the Church. Frequently they imagine that the Church is a tyrannical and bossy mother who capriciously orders people about and in so doing corrupts the freedom Christ came to offer. They don't want to be guided by an institution that they think "makes up" rules so as to keep discipline in the ranks.

But the Church makes no such claim. Her doctrines come from Christ who gives his Church the Spirit. She can exercise her authority only in the name and manner of Christ, not despotically "lording it over others" but serving them.[4] In fact, the Latin word *auctoritas* comes from the word meaning to further something in its growth. Possessing all power on heaven and earth, Jesus was among us as one who serves (cf. Mark 10:42-44). The Church must do likewise. He insisted: "Whoever wants to be first must be last of all and servant of all" (Mark 9:36).

Apostolic Servants of Truth

Who in the Church fulfills this role of servant teacher? Jesus entrusted to his most intimate disciples, the Twelve, the particular ministry of teaching his message in its integrity. The bishops, with the Pope, continue this original apostolic ministry so that the truth of revelation, "according to his good pleasure that he set forth in Christ" (Ephesians 1:9), can be faithfully taught in every generation: preserved from corruption, defended from error, proposed to meet new challenges.[5]

The first and primary apostle, the "one sent," is the Son. In addressing the Father, Jesus said: "As you have sent me into the world, so I have sent them into the world" (John 17:18). On Easter evening he divulged his will to his apostles: "As the Father has sent me, so am I sending you" (John 20:21). In the world of Jesus, people understand that the one who sends is present in the one sent: "The Father is in me and I am in the Father" (John 10:38). Just as Jesus is the Father's instrument, so are his apostles the ones through whom he continues his redeeming work in the world.

This original apostolic group is a linchpin because Jesus shared with them his own *exousia* (from the Greek for "authority"), which is the basis of all pastoral authority in the Church. When he said to the Twelve, "Whatever you bind on earth will be bound in heaven, and whatever you loose on earth will be loosed in heaven" (Matthew 18:18), Jesus gave them the authority to teach his truth. Those entrusted with this apostolic ministry can discern between true and false teaching.

Successors to the Apostles

As far as we can determine, Jesus never explicitly mentioned the need for co-workers or successors to the Twelve. Yet there are good reasons for interpreting that his commission to the apostles implied cooperators and, later, successors. In order for the Gospel to be heard, a preacher is needed, since "faith comes from what is heard" (Romans 10:17). St. Paul understood the dynamic well: "And how are they [unbelievers] to hear without someone to proclaim him? And how are they to proclaim him unless they are sent?" (Romans 10:14-15). Since by Jesus' order, the Gospel is to be proclaimed until the end of time (cf. Matthew 28:18-20), this unquestionably implies that others must teach and baptize even after the apostles had died. Those others — the bishops — succeed to the ministry of the apostles.

Christ intended the Church to survive in the form in which he had established her. When communities were without the authority of an apostle, they still had to be able to continue to function according to Christ's will for his community. With the passing away of the apostolic generation, the community realized its need to preserve the unity of faith entrusted to it. According to God's plan, successors emerged. Vatican II describes this apostolic succession: "In order that the mission assigned to them might continue after their death, they [the apostles] passed on to their immediate cooperators, as it were, in the form of a testament, the duty of confirming and finishing the work begun by themselves . . . they therefore appointed such men, and gave them the order that, when they should have died, other approved men would take up their ministry."[6] Because Christ willed that this office of nurturing the Church be permanent, Vatican II teaches that "bishops by divine institution have succeeded to the place of apostles, as shepherds of the Church."[7]

God's offer of salvation reaches us through the encounter of a preacher and a hearer of the word. The Church's structure is built on persons. Christ entrusted his message to people, not to a book. Ministry is never self-conferred or bestowed by the community. It is offered to those who succeed to the ministry first conferred by Christ and empowered by the Spirit.[8] Fundamental to Catholicism is the principle that Christ's personal presence in the Church is conveyed through living ministers who continue to represent him.

Among the charisms (or special gifts) the early Church received from the Spirit were those of apostle, prophet, pastor, and teacher (cf. 1 Corinthians 12:28). The first Christian communities accepted that bishops had the determinative role, like the apostles, in teaching and settling disputes, precisely because they were authoritative witnesses to the apostolic tradition. By the mid-second century, bishops were established throughout the Church as heads of local communities and were considered to have succeeded to the place of the apostles. At the turn of the third century, Tertullian expressed common Church teaching on the apostolic succession of bishops: "It follows that all doctrine which agrees with the apostolic churches, those nurseries and original depositories of the faith, must be regarded as truth, and as undoubtedly constituting what the churches received from the apostles, what the apostles received from Christ, and what Christ received from God."[9]

The identity of the apostolic faith is preserved through this succession of office, and the bishops succeed to the mission of the apostles. Though not eyewitnesses to Jesus' public ministry and paschal mystery, bishops remain the guardians of the deposit of faith. St. Paul's admonition to St. Timothy bears witness to this obligation: "Guard the good treasure entrusted to you, with the help of the Holy Spirit living in us" (2 Timothy 1:14; cf. 1 Timothy 6:20; 2 Timothy 1:12).

God's word of revelation is preserved and transmitted to us in Scripture and sacred tradition. As we have seen, just as these two cannot be separated from each other, neither can they be separated from the Church's living teaching authority, her *magisterium.*[10] Vatican II is clear on this point: "The duty, however, of authentically interpreting the Word of God, whether written or handed down, has been given only to the living magisterium of the Church whose authority is exercised in the name of Jesus Christ."[11] The Holy Spirit guarantees this handing on of divine revelation. Consequently, the Church preserves the same faith from the apostolic age to the present.

Although everyone has a duty to submit to the truth, within the Church only bishops officially proclaim it in the name of Christ. They do not speak on their own behalf. That's why bishops are not representatives of the people or consensus managers.

Teaching Authority

This teaching office of the successors to the apostles is essential to the Church. If she is to discern reliably what Scripture and tradition mean, what belongs to the deposit of faith and what is venerable (though changeable) custom, she needs the magisterium.

Jesus was passionate about the truth, describing himself as not only "the way and the life" but also "the truth" (cf. John 14:6). He dedicated most of his public ministry to preparing his apostles for their mission and sharing with them the truth he enjoyed from the Father.

Since all revealed religion is based on the absolute truth of God's word, the role of any human mediator is to help others come to know that word.[12] By the power of the Spirit, the bishops are equipped to communicate God's saving plan as it was revealed — truthfully, though not exhaustively. Bishops have the duty of guaranteeing that Catholics receive the "real thing," the same glad tidings preached by the apostles — and not some diluted Gospel adapted to the spirit of the age. By what right do the bishops teach with the authority of Christ? Assuredly not their own holiness or their theological expertise. Rather, God has given them a special gift of the Spirit to speak with authority. Not politicians who can adjust their "policies" to fit their followers' fancies, bishops are preachers of the salvation received from Christ and believed by the Catholic Church.

By belonging to the Catholic Church we accept our bishops as authentic teachers endowed with Christ's authority. "The duty of the faithful to obey the authority of the pastors," wrote Pope Paul VI, "is an essential requirement of the very nature of Christianity."[13] Among the bishops' primary concerns is orthodoxy, that is, maintaining the purity of the faith to which they bear witness and which they hand on. They must also faithfully interpret the demands of the Gospel for today's Church. Not relying on mere verbal orthodoxy, the bishops are to apply the power of the truth to their communities, "in a manner adapted to the needs of the times, that is to say, in a manner corresponding to the difficulties and problems by which people are most vexatiously burdened and troubled."[14]

We need bishops to tell us unambiguously the Gospel truth. Within the believing community they have the final responsibility for its preservation. They alone can authorize, before the whole Church, new definitions of faith. Only they have the right to judge what is to be taught as the teaching of Christ and the apostles. In matters of salvation, we need a court of appeal for decisions. Were it not for the bishops, we would not know which books make up sacred Scripture, whether the Son is "begotten" or "made," or whether confirmation is a sacrament! Their solemn teachings defined at ecumenical councils have preserved us in the truth.

Without these spokesmen, Jesus' truth would never have reached to the ends of the world. At best, we would have access today to what people might have thought Christ had said. Subsequent generations would not have received saving revelation but a series of opinions. What I want is the truth of Christ, not the erroneous beliefs of misguided preachers with good intentions. Through her bishops the Catholic Church assures me that I can confront the genuine teaching of Christ. Their magisterium "must protect God's people from the danger of deviations and confusion, guaranteeing them the objective possibility of professing the authentic faith free from error, at all times and in diverse situations."[15]

Docility to the Magisterium

Let's face it. It's not easy for us to accept a real teaching authority. We are chafed by its claim. A couple of reasons are behind this unease. First, the modern mind has grown up with ideas of emancipation and liberation from any authority. "Seeing for yourself, thinking for yourself, judging for yourself, and having the courage to use your own reason," writes Walter Kasper, "is part of the fundamental attitude of enlightened modern men and women."[16] The second reason revolves around two movements of contemporary philosophy. Although most of us do not consider ourselves philosophers, we are still affected by their ideas. Existentialism, for instance, focuses on the unique human person for whom authoritative teaching, which is meant for all, is seen as alien. Critical rationalism says that truth can never really be attained but only pursued.[17] In simple terms, this is reduced to: "My opinion is as good as yours." Teaching authority, which would favor a particular view, is thus conceived as an enemy of openness. With this cultural baggage no wonder people find it difficult to accept the magisterium!

Belonging to the Church entails obedience to her.[18] Despite its negative press as paternalistic or unfit for "adult" Christians, obedience is necessary for those who want to follow in the Master's footsteps. If Christ was not ashamed to be "obedient to the point of death" (Philippians 2:8), how can we expect not to be obedient? Christian freedom makes sense only in light of Christ's freedom. Catholics are called to be as obedient to the body of Christ as Christ himself was to the Father. Docility goes hand-in-hand with freedom. Christ's authority lives in the Church's ministers. To show them love and obedience saves turning their office into a bureaucracy which one could only deplore and criticize.[19]

In everyday life we obey, even if reluctantly, because we acknowledge a superior's competence. In the Church we trust that the Lord himself has guaranteed that his teaching will be kept undefiled through the ministry he established. Because of our faith in him, we ought to obey those with whom he has shared his authority. We should not, therefore, treat Church teaching as if it were an imposed set of social standards, more or less arbitrary, which are akin to civil law.

Docility to episcopal and papal teaching does not do away with the need to offer necessary constructive criticism of persons or institutions in the Church. Yet such criticism should be offered with charity, and where remedies can be applied, not theatrically and in public.[20]

Christians are called to be "children of God" (1 John 3:1). That is what we are. We are to live this childhood as adults, always remembering that we owe our existence to Another and that we must give thanks for that. Although popular lingo now favors the expression that we "celebrate" the sacraments, it is equally true to say that we "receive" them. This latter usage calls to mind that before the Giver of all gifts we are all dependent children. Similarly, before the Church's official proclamation of her faith, we are like children who frequently do not understand. For this reason, we must be careful not to let our own inability to grasp an authoritative teaching impede our accepting it.

Bishops are called pastors or shepherds because they lead us. Yet "the pastoral image of the sheep that are led to pasture does not indicate immaturity, but rather the docility of even mature Christians."[21] Only because of the eternal Son's exemplary docility and obedience can Christians defend themselves against the charge that they are minors without responsibility.[22]

Society has made us suspicious about entrusting ourselves to anyone, let alone to the Church. Yet this entrusting is at the heart of faith. If, however, we take our cues from our political and social culture, then almost inevitably, our reception of Church teaching is conditioned by our understanding of their structures: the governed have a right to be consulted on all matters of common concern; just rule is by majority vote; personal rights are jealously guarded. These cultural assumptions are powerful indeed, and they predispose us to think of Church teaching in the same way. Fortunately the Lord gave us the means to override our cultural prejudices by leaving us the apostolic ministry, inviting us to imitate Christ's obedience by our own docility.

In *The Splendour of the Church*, among the great Catholic

books of the twentieth century, Henri de Lubac explains the vitality of a Catholic's freely offered obedience to the Church: "History and his own experience combine to show him [the man of the Church] both the desire for the knowledge of divine things which stirs the human spirit, and the weakness which lays that spirit open to falling into every kind of error. In consequence, he appreciates the benefit of the divine magisterium, to which he freely submits. He thanks God for having given him that magisterium in the Church, and experiences a foretaste of the peace of eternity in placing himself under the eternal law by the obedience of faith."[23]

Guaranteed Teaching: Work of the Holy Spirit

CATHOLICS HAVE A SENSE OF SURETY ABOUT THEIR FAITH THAT many envy and find attractive. Others, however, are more put off than attracted by the Church's claim to infallible truth, linking it to oppression of conscience, the Inquisition, intolerance, and rigidity.[1]

The Church presents a core of beliefs that Catholics are required to believe. Such beliefs are taught "infallibly"; that is, they are free from error. When the Church puts her full authority behind a specific teaching, she cannot deceive us about what to believe or how to live. In these statements she shares in Christ's own truthfulness. The Spirit speaks the truth in love to the Church (cf. Ephesians 4:15).

This guidance of the Spirit is not limited, however, to assisting the magisterium when it teaches infallibly. The divine plan is not only that "everyone be saved" but also that everyone may "come to the knowledge of the truth" (1 Timothy 2:4). Most of the Church's teaching is of a more ordinary sort. As authoritative, it too preserves "the truth of the gospel" (Galatians 2:5) for God's people but without the absolute certitude of infallibly proposed teaching.

Infallibility: Extraordinary Gift

I belong to the Church that will remain in existence, faithful to the Gospel, until the end of time. This Church will never put the full weight of her authority behind a teaching that she will later reverse because it is outdated or false. What the Church solemnly proposes as true teaching, as divinely revealed, cannot be erroneous — despite the inadequacy of how she may sometimes teach it. You will not wake up some morning and read in the newspaper that the Church has dropped her teaching on the indissolubility of marriage. Nor will the news media ever report that the Pope has decided that Mary was never assumed into heaven.

Such a gift could only come from God. From the apostolic age onward, we Christians have been convinced that Jesus is with us, faithful to his promise to send the Spirit of Truth from the Father (cf. John 15:26, 14:16-17). This Spirit guides the community "into all the truth" (John 16:13) and saves "the church of the living God, the pillar and bulwark of the truth" (1 Timothy 3:15) from binding Catholics to believe false doctrine. The root of infallibility is "in the fidelity of the Spirit: he cannot abandon God's chosen ones to falsehood."[2]

The Church's pastors have never proposed as a dogma of faith any teaching that contradicts the Gospel. Believing that the Church is usually on track or that, despite serious errors here and there in her dogma, she has remained on the right road does not do justice to Catholic teaching. To hold that there can be true errors in infallibly proposed teaching is incompatible with the Church's faith.[3]

A couple of common misunderstandings should be cleared up at the outset. This gift makes no claim regarding the personal sinlessness of bishops and the Pope. Nor is it equivalent to inspiration, the charism given to the biblical authors so "that the books of Scripture, firmly, faithfully and without error, teach that truth which God, for the sake of our salvation, wished to see confided to the sacred Scriptures."[4]

In his *Essay on the Development of Christian Doctrine* (1878 edition), John Henry Newman presented a compelling argument explaining why the Church must be able to teach without error. Catholicism is founded on the fact that God has revealed his truth to us in Jesus. This truth was accurately preserved in the apostolic preaching. Since its accuracy must be maintained through time, if the Church is to preserve her divinely given identity, some means must be available that can uphold this truth unblemished when it is threatened. Through the centuries disputes have arisen among believers. When this happens, how do we know which opinion preserves the truth? According to Cardinal Newman, we can distinguish truth from error in this case because the Church enjoys a supreme authority supported by a divine guarantee. In certain circumstances, pastors in the Church can rely upon God's special help to teach the truth without error. Without this guarantee the Church could err, and the gates of hell would have prevailed against her (cf. Matthew 16:19). Therefore, an infallible magisterium not only makes sense, there could be no preaching of Christ, the "same yesterday and today and forever" without it (Hebrews 13:8)!

Infallibility does not rest upon human factors of intelligence, shrewdness, or political maneuvering. Though these may condition *how* or *when* a certain dogma is formulated, they do not determine its truth. As the highest degree of participation in Christ's authority, infallibility is not given for the Church's self-aggrandizement but for preaching the Gospel in its integrity.[5] Infallibility is a special assistance that enables the Church to understand rightly divine revelation.

Infallibility of the Whole Church

In the first place, God gives infallibility to the whole Church as a believing community. Nothing is more traditional than St. Robert Bellarmine's teaching that "what all the faithful hold as a matter of faith is necessarily true and of faith." The reason for this confidence is the Holy Spirit who interiorly helps believers to embrace the truth and reject error. Because the Protestant Reformers so emphasized the "interior testimony of the Holy Spirit" as the criterion of biblical truth, for a long time Catholics minimized the infallibility of the whole Church in believing. Instead she emphasized the special role of her official teachers.

In *On Consulting the Faithful in Matters of Doctrine* (1859), Cardinal Newman analyzed this "instinct" of the faithful. Their sense of the faith has both preserved the Gospel's truth, as in the fourth-century Arian crisis, and has led to a dogmatic formulation, as occurred when Pius IX defined the Immaculate Conception in 1854. Much inspired by Newman, the Council Fathers at Vatican II made use of his idea when they stated: "The whole body of the faithful who have an anointing that comes from the holy one . . . cannot err in matters of belief."[6] They thereby made clear that the Catholic faith belongs to the whole Church, not to any group within her.

This infallibility of the believing community is not, however, an ecclesiastical variant of majority rule. Everyone's "opinion" is not worth the same as everyone else's! Polling those who claim to be Catholic about the Church's faith is not an index to truth. A very important qualification must be kept in mind, though pollsters systematically ignore it. God promises his gift of infallibility to *believers*, that is, to those who open themselves to Christ and his Spirit and are living in full communion with the Church — practicing Catholics. Those who cling to private beliefs or who identify only partially with the Church cannot lay claim to this infallibility in believing. St. Augustine says that this gift is present only when all those, "from the bishops to the last members of the faithful," accept a particular teaching.[7] The bottom line? Playing off the infallibility of the whole Church against episcopal and papal teaching is a dead end. Lobby groups can't invoke their "infallibility" to present the Pope and bishops with petitions about doctrines they want changed and expect a hearing.

Who Can Teach Infallibly?

The whole Church possesses the truth, but authoritatively proclaiming it is not the equal responsibility of everyone. This charge rests with those whom Christ has mandated, the bishops.

He willed that the bishops, whom he entrusted with his truth, be endowed with the gift of teaching infallibly in matters of faith and morals.

Every bishop is obliged to maintain the unity of faith. But he can teach infallibly only when he is in full communion with his brother bishops, including the Pope, either at an ecumenical council or when dispersed throughout the world. The Pope alone can also teach a doctrine infallibly to the whole Church.[8]

Bishops at Ecumenical Councils • On twenty-one different occasions in the Church's history, most recently at the Second Vatican Council (1962-1965), large gatherings of bishops from the whole world have come together to deal with major doctrinal, disciplinary, and pastoral questions affecting the universal Church. Such assemblies are extraordinary moments in Catholic life, usually called to resolve disputes that have arisen. To settle these controversies, the bishops, with the Pope's approval, render a definitive judgment. When these Fathers are gathered together at an ecumenical council, they act as "teachers and judges of faith and morals for the universal Church." Consequently, when the bishops, in union with the Pope, call upon the Spirit to settle a doctrinal controversy, "their definitions must then be adhered to with the submission of faith."[9] In this instance, they are teaching infallibly.

To avoid any ambiguity about whether they are defining a matter of faith or morals, the bishops at a council declare *anathema* anyone who rejects their teaching. Those who do not accept the conciliar definition are "separated" from the believing community because they no longer share its faith. To reject the infallibly proposed teaching of an ecumenical council is heresy. Not everything bishops agree to at a council is of course infallibly taught. At Vatican II, for instance, the bishops did not define any new dogma of Catholic faith.

Bishops United Throughout the World • As crucial as the definitive teaching of ecumenical councils often is, such events have taken place on the average of about once a century. Can the bishops teach infallibly at any other time? Yes, they can. Even when they are not assembled at an ecumenical council, Catholic bishops can proclaim the Gospel to us without error. Theologians and Church documents call this the *universal ordinary magisterium.*[10]

In a frequently overlooked text of the Second Vatican Council, the Fathers explained the conditions that had to be met for such teaching to be considered infallible: "Although the individual bishops do not enjoy the prerogative of infallibility, they do, nevertheless, enunciate the doctrine of Christ infallibly when, even dispersed around the world but preserving the bond of communion between themselves and with the successor of Peter, they concur on one judgment as having to be held definitively, while authentically teaching on matters of faith and morals."[11]

Though this way of teaching infallibly is often ignored, it is the normal means the Spirit uses for preserving and spreading the integrity of the apostolic faith. When it is certain that a teaching is infallibly proposed by the universal ordinary magisterium, then Catholics are obliged to give it the assent of faith. The motive for believing this teaching is divine authority itself. Among the dogmas falling into this category are Jesus' bodily resurrection, Mary's perpetual virginity, and the grave moral evil of directly taking innocent human life.

How do you know in a particular instance whether the college of bishops, with the Pope, has fulfilled all the conditions for teaching infallibly in this way? I can suggest a *practical guideline.* Since the Pope's assent to any such teaching is absolutely necessary, Catholics can look to his magisterium for guidance in this matter. As head of the college of bishops, he acts as their spokesman in proclaiming the Church's faith.

When all the conditions mentioned in *Lumen Gentium* are met, such teaching, which renders a definitive judgment, is infallibly proposed. It is free from error, not as an *ex cathedra* definition, but because all bishops teach it. A clear example of this is the Pope's repeated defense of human life by his condemnation of direct abortion. I believe that such teaching is infallible because it meets all the conditions set out by the Second Vatican Council. Even if a future council or papal statement were to propose it solemnly, they would only be ratifying what is already infallibly taught.

The Pope • The bishop of Rome, as successor of Peter, enjoys a primacy of teaching in the Church. It is his special responsibility to shield Christ's flock "from the poisoned food of error."[12] At the First Vatican Council in 1870, the Fathers maintained that the Pope could not carry out his mission to the flock entrusted to him by Jesus (cf. John 21:15-17) unless his teaching, when necessary, was guaranteed to be free from error. In *Pastor Aeternus*, they stated unequivocally that such a charism of truth was "conferred by God on Peter and his successors."[13]

Among all the bishops, only the Pope enjoys this fullness of teaching authority in his own name. No other bishop in the Church can claim this prerogative. At Vatican I the Fathers defined papal infallibility as follows: "It is a divinely revealed dogma that the Roman Pontiff, when he speaks *ex cathedra*, that is, when, acting in the office of shepherd and teacher of all Christians, he defines, by virtue of his supreme apostolic authority, a doctrine concerning faith or morals to be held by the universal Church, possesses through the divine assistance promised to him in the person of Blessed Peter, the infallibility with which the divine Redeemer willed his Church to be endowed in defining the doctrine concerning faith or morals; and that such definitions of the Roman Pontiff are therefore irreformable of themselves, not because of the consent of the Church."[14]

Since God promises this charism for a specific purpose, the Pope can use it only if he meets specific conditions. First, he must act as shepherd and teacher of all Christians, and not as a private theologian. Second, the Pope must put the entire weight of his Petrine ministry behind what he says; he is not acting as bishop of the diocese of Rome or as patriarch of the West. Third, papal infallibility attaches only to the specific teaching of a particular pope, who teaches it explicitly and freely. No teaching is infallible simply because it is repeated by a long series of popes. Fourth, the Holy Father must have a genuine intention to define a matter of faith or morals so that it calls for Catholics to give their assent of faith. Lastly, the Pope must clearly invoke his supreme teaching authority in such a way that it is obvious to the Church that he is doing so. No doubt should exist whether the Pope is using his charism to teach infallibly. The *Code of Canon Law* states that "no doctrine is understood to be infallibly defined unless this is manifestly demonstrated."[15] When these conditions are all satisfied, the Holy Father teaches *ex cathedra*, or infallibly — that is, from the *cathedra* or throne of Peter whose successor he is.

What Can Be Taught Infallibly?

According to both Vatican I and Vatican II, the divine Redeemer willed that the gift of infallibility should extend "as far as the deposit of divine revelation extends, which must be religiously guarded and faithfully expounded."[16]

Catholics accept that the bishops and Pope can teach infallibly on matters of faith and morals. The Church's pastors can make a definitive judgment about questions of faith — for example, that Jesus Christ is "one-in-being with the Father" (defined at the Council of Nicaea in 325) or that Mary was assumed body and soul into heaven (defined *ex cathedra* by Pope

Pius XII in 1950). Moral matters also fall within the scope of the Church's competence to teach infallibly. This is so, even if the Scriptures do not deal with them explicitly. Questions such as contraception and abortion, and undoubtedly others that will later arise, *can* be proposed infallibly. According to Vatican II, the competence of the Church's teaching authority extends to the natural law: "The Church is, by the will of Christ, the teacher of the truth. It is her duty to give utterance to, and authoritatively to teach, that Truth which is Christ Himself, and also to declare and confirm by her authority those principles of the moral order that have their origin in human nature itself."[17]

The *Catechism of the Catholic Church* clearly reaffirms the magisterium's competence to teach infallibly on specific precepts of the natural law.[18] Bishops have "the task of discerning, by means of judgments normative for the consciences of believers, those acts which in themselves conform to the demands of faith and foster their expression in life and those which, on the contrary, because [they are] intrinsically evil, are incompatible with such demands."[19]

Belonging to the Church gives Catholics a taste of truth's victory over falsehood — a triumph that Jesus promised to his Church. So as to guard and faithfully expound the Gospel, the bishops and Pope enjoy, in the three situations mentioned, the special assistance of the Holy Spirit who preserves Christ's Church from error in her teaching.

Authoritative Teaching: Ordinary Gift

In the contemporary world, rubber hits the religious road most obviously on moral questions. With a few notable exceptions, such as abortion and euthanasia, neither bishops nor the Pope have taught infallibly in the tortuous domain of morals. Does this mean they must keep demurely silent? By no means! Normally the Pope and the other bishops, individually and collectively, teach the faith in a way that is *authoritative*, without invoking the charism of infallibility.[20]

Since the bishops exercise their authority in the name of Christ, let's look at how the Lord dealt with moral questions. Jesus' contemporaries did not hesitate to ask him for his views on how to live. "Teacher, we know that you are right in what you say and teach, and you show deference to no one, but teach the way of God in accordance with truth" (Luke 20:21). Not at all reticent, he never deflected their serious moral questions with an evasive "No comment." He told them — and us — what he thought concerning divorce, forgiveness, and paying taxes to Caesar. Nor did St. Paul hesitate to teach the first Christian communities about how they were to conduct themselves once baptized into Christ Jesus. Similarly the bishops and Pope teach on moral matters integral to Christian living. Think what would happen if they were silent on such matters. The Gospel that they preach would touch few of the problems that most preoccupy us — a sure recipe for irrelevance.

The bishops and Pope receive the gift of the Spirit to preach with authority. God has chosen them to be teachers in his Church. Not politicians who can adjust their "policies" to fit their followers' fancies, they teach authoritatively the message of salvation revealed by Christ and believed by the Catholic Church. In their repeated teaching on questions such as remarriage after divorce, homosexual acts, and the need for private confession, they are not merely offering their personal opinions on topical issues. On the contrary, they are instructing Catholics how to form their consciences and so act with the light of the Gospel.[21] To belong to the Catholic Church is to give ear to the apostles' teaching in the bishops' voices.

Best Available Guide

By acknowledging the Catholic Church as my teacher, I recognize that her authoritative (but not infallibly proposed) teaching deserves to be accepted as a sure guide in religious and moral questions. To do so is neither irresponsible nor immature.

Just because a particular teaching is not guaranteed by the charism of infallibility does not mean that it is either just a high-level ecclesiastical opinion or an open question. It may be "as certain as any natural truth,"[22] though not confirmed by the absolute guarantee of infallibility. What the Pope and bishops propose authoritatively, but noninfallibly, is very *probably* true.[23] In the future, such a teaching may need reformulation or correction. For the present, however, this authoritative teaching is the *best* guide we have in order to know what Christ thinks about a particular question.

A reasonable person follows the best teacher available at the time. What better teachers has the Lord provided than the bishops? Surely not theologians, religious educators, media celebrities, or even parish priests. The Church's authoritative teaching therefore deserves the presumption of truth. To disregard it or treat it as one opinion among many shows a lack of docility to those who hold the place of successors to the apostles. Furthermore, it is less reasonable to follow the possibly erroneous judgments of other authorities — unless of course they are endowed with the infallibility that they deny to the magisterium! Following the authoritative magisterium is therefore the most prudent course of action for a Catholic who wants to live in communion with Christ.

Such docile prudence is confirmed by daily experience. In our everyday life, we constantly act with less than absolute certitude about whether a given action is right. Doctors, for example, must routinely make diagnostic decisions without absolute certainty. Yet we follow them, knowing that they might be mistaken. Given their expertise, they are the best judges of our medical situation at this time. In the same way, the magisterium must teach on important issues even if it is not (yet) able to render a definitive judgment.

If she is to preach the Gospel powerfully in a constantly and fast-changing world, the Church cannot allow herself to be immobilized by remaining silent on controversial issues. Not teaching because the conditions for infallibility are lacking would be dereliction of duty.[24] The ordinary magisterium applies the Gospel to real-life situations. Do we not desperately need the community's guidance in such questions as genetic manipulation, surrogate motherhood, or nuclear deterrence? Christ has entrusted his Church with teachers who, even when not invoking infallibility, are neither to remain dumb nor to be treated merely as religious consultants offering occasional advice.

Catholics should strive to form their conscience according to such authoritative teaching, though the assent of divine faith, which is given only to what is divinely revealed, is not called for. At all costs, they must avoid thinking that this "noninfallible" teaching is somehow "optional." Belief in the trustworthiness of the bishops' teaching ministry is essential to one's Catholic life.

Official Papal Teaching

Vatican II singles out the Pope's authoritative magisterium for special attention because of its particular role in Catholic life. If the Pope's teaching ministry were limited to those extraordinary occasions when he speaks *ex cathedra*, then since 1950 no Pope would have had anything at all to teach us! Clearly, then, papal teaching authority involves more than once-a-century pronouncements. Why would Catholics — and others — listen so closely to his teaching on humanitarian interventions involving the use of arms, human rights, the exclusion of women from the ministerial priesthood, and so many other issues, if he was only dispensing fatherly advice?

Although every Pope, including John Paul II, has his own theological opinions, he cannot impose these on the universal

Church. Catholics distinguish a Pope's personal views from his authoritative teaching. Even if the former is interesting and instructive, it does not call a Catholic to obedience. Yet, according to Vatican II, "religious submission of mind and will must be shown in a special way to the authentic [authoritative] magisterium of the Roman Pontiff, even when he is not speaking *ex cathedra*."[25] Such assent is called "religious submission" because "it is an exercise of virtue whose motive is ultimately directed to Christ, from whom the pastors of the Church have received their authority and in whose name they preach."[26]

This "religious submission of mind and will" means more than having a respectful attitude toward the Church's teachers and a concern for preserving unity. When a Catholic gives religious submission of mind and will to authoritative papal teaching, he or she recognizes that such teaching might belong to revelation, even if this has not yet been determined.[27]

If a recent clothing catalog can advertise its "almost infallible guide" to match snazzy ties with properly coordinated shirts, it is not creeping "papolatry" to suggest that the Pope's authoritative non-*ex cathedra* teaching might make an equal claim! It would not be rash to recognize that this teaching corresponds to the Gospel. In his ordinary magisterium, the Pope teaches with the authority of Christ. Reasonable, prudent, and loyal Catholics will accept this authoritative papal magisterium as a certain guide in forming their conscience.

Catholic teaching on infallibility is often misinterpreted as human arrogance, as guaranteeing a security that belongs only to the heavenly kingdom. Yet I believe it is a precious gift bestowed so that we "may stand mature and fully assured in everything that God wills" (Colossians 4:12). He gives us his truth so that we might be sanctified through it (cf. John 17:17).

In the Church's certain teaching, we have a foretaste of Christ's definitive victory over "the father of lies" (John 8:44). The Lord gives us this "assured understanding" so that we might "have the knowledge of God's mystery, that is, Christ himself, in whom are hidden all the treasures of wisdom and knowledge" (Colossians 2:2).

Because of her infallibility, the Church is protected from the dangers of deviation and confusion. By God's grace she can profess her faith free from error always and everywhere. Infallibility guarantees that the Church will not succumb to the temptations to reinterpret the Gospel according to her wants, needs, or interests. It is through the Spirit's unfailing fidelity to the Church that the wisdom of God is preserved and proclaimed for us.

The One Full Church

INEVITABLY THOSE INTERESTED IN THE CHURCH COME UP AGAINST *the* question: "What about the Catholic claim to be the 'true Church,' the one founded by Jesus?" Just as Jesus claimed to be the Son of God and challenged those following him to acknowledge him as Lord, the Catholic Church's affirmation to be the true Church forces one to examine this claim, "as outrageous as it is unavoidable."[1] If it is not true, it can be dismissed as the most arrogant claim imaginable; but if it is true, then any honest person must take whatever steps are necessary to live in harmony with that truth.

Catholics do not settle for some vague adherence to Jesus' teachings. They insist that the fullness of Christianity is found only by belonging to the Church. Because the Church herself is necessary, "denominational preference" is therefore not a secondary but a *primary* question. Catholics are not indifferent to whether one is Lutheran, Baptist, or Episcopalian. Somehow, often in ways that are not well expressed, they believe that it is "better" to be Catholic.

Why Is the Church Necessary?

Americans pride themselves on being individualists. They are inventive, self-reliant, and — at least in principle — stubbornly resist being dictated to by others. When lived in light of Christ's teachings, these traits produce the good fruit of responsibility. Yet they can also lead to accepting values contrary to those found in the Gospel. When the autonomous individual, divorced from larger communities, reigns supreme, freedom and autonomy are limited only by freely entered into "contracts." Slogans such as "I'm my own boss" or "No one can tell me what to do with my body" capture this spirit. In street language, you can do whatever you want as long as no one gets hurt. Pope John Paul II speaks of this corruption of freedom as "an autonomous power of self-affirmation, often against others, for one's own selfish well-being."[2] It is really a kind of slavery to the isolated self.

Given this spirit, it is no wonder that sects and endless splinter churches, where each person is armed with a Bible to be privately interpreted, have enjoyed such success in America. As anything more than a fellowship of like-minded believers, the Church for them is optional. How often have you heard people announce that they can be "good *Christians*" without going to Church? This attitude troubles me for two reasons. First, I wonder how they can be so certain about their own goodness. I think the pursuit of holiness is much more difficult, exciting, and mysterious. Second, I question where they get the idea of a churchless Christianity. That position turns the Gospel into a compendium of tips for successful living from a wise man who can offer some helpful advice. Yet Jesus is alive, working in his Church.

Belonging to the Church is not like joining a country club. You might or might not have the interest, money, or time for such leisure. In any case, you're a member only if and for as long as you want to be. Those who do decide to join a club are selective and search out precisely what they want in prestige, activities, and cost. What happens when the same criteria are applied to joining a church? The result is that people "shop for the best package deal they can get, and when they find a better deal they have little hesitation about switching."[3] For many, belonging to a church is too readily compared to hunting for a bargain. Catholics, however, see matters differently.

We *need* the Church. This need does not spring arbitrarily from Jesus' will, as if he tacked on the Church as an afterthought to his message. Rather, the Lord created us so that in our religious and spiritual life we need to express ourselves as social beings. The human person is inherently social, called "from the innermost depths of self to *communion* with others and to the *giving* of self to others."[4] The same can be said of the Church. Our fellowship with the Holy Trinity, the life of grace, is lived in fellowship or communion with others (cf. 1 John 1:3).

God's relationship to us, and our relationship to God, is therefore not exclusively or even primarily individualistic. Taking place in the community, it is corporate and communal. Just as all humanity sinned "in Adam" (cf. Romans 5:12), so have we been redeemed "in Christ," the New Adam. For Catholics, this community is the people of God of the New Covenant, the Church.

God himself created the Church to be the means of salvation through Jesus Christ. She is the chosen instrument by which all humanity is led back to its Creator: from the "one" Christ, through the "one" Church, for the "one" eternal life. As Christ directed his mission to all, so does the Church. She brings salvation to the whole world as the visible instrument or sacrament of its redemption.[5]

Catholics recognize that the Church exists because of Christ. He remains her head and heart. The Church's task is to bring about and foster communion between Christ and the individual. She enables each person to find Christ, in order that he may walk with "each person the path of life, with the power of the truth about man and the world that is contained in the mystery of the incarnation and the Redemption and with the power of the love that is radiated by that truth."[6]

Claim to Be the "True" Church

Despite the ecumenical embarrassment, Catholics believe that the Catholic Church is the true Church established by Christ, the one founded by Jesus on Peter and the apostles. No official document published before or since Vatican II compromises this essential teaching. What we can discover in the conciliar, papal, and episcopal magisterium, however, is a growing appreciation of the saving significance of other churches, Christian communities, and religious groups not in communion with the Pope.

The Fathers at Vatican II affirmed that "the Church established by Christ the Lord is, indeed, one and unique."[7] Baptism is the sacrament of incorporation into this one Church of Christ that is historically present in the Catholic Church: "This is the one Church of Christ which in the Creed is professed as one, holy, catholic and apostolic, which our Savior, after his resurrection, commissioned Peter to shepherd. . . . This Church [of Christ] constituted and organized in the world as a society, subsists in the Catholic Church, which is governed by the successor of Peter. . . ."[8]

Catholic believers continue to hold resolutely that Christianity is not only true, but also that it exists fully only in the Catholic Church. They claim that she has received, by divine providence, a *fullness* of revealed truth, sacramental life, and pastoral ministry that is at least partially lacking in every other Christian church or ecclesial community. Two doctrines are at stake in this claim: first, that Jesus established only *one* Church; second, that this one Church, the Catholic Church, is the *full* Church.

Why the Church Is One

To belong to the Catholic Church, then, is to belong to the one Church founded by our Lord himself. Several reasons can be given for this oneness — why there are not different churches, each of which has an equal claim to be this one Church. First, we have scriptural justification: the promise of Christ and the biblical images used for the community. Second, we have arguments based on theological fittingness — that is, reasons that make sense of this oneness in light of other truths: the mystery of the Trinity and Jesus as our one mediator.

Were there more than one Church, then there would be more than one faith, contrary to Jesus' undeniable desire that his disciples "may all be one" (John 17:21). Furthermore, think of St. Paul's testimony: There is only "one Lord, one faith, one baptism, one God and Father of all" (Ephesians 4:5). To deny that the Catholic Church is the one Church of Jesus Christ would come down to saying that Jesus had willed different churches with contradictory beliefs!

The Catholic Church understands herself as radically "one," just as we profess in the Nicene Creed. In the Scriptures, the Church is repeatedly described as one. She is the one vine that has Christ as its trunk (cf. John 15:1-8), the one kingdom that is not divided against itself (cf. Matthew 12:25), the one flock that has one shepherd (cf. John 10:16), the one bride that has Christ as her spouse (cf. Ephesians 5:22-33), and the one body that has Christ as its head (cf. Ephesians 1:22). There is only one Church — and the Catholic Church so sees herself, unambiguously and serenely.

When we look even more closely at the Scriptures, this oneness of the Church depends on Jesus, the one and only "mediator between God and humankind" (1 Timothy 2:5). Christ, the Word made flesh, reconciled all people to God by the cross and restored humanity's unity in one people and one body.[9] Non-Catholic Christians themselves are divided. Not so Christ's Church. Her oneness follows from that of Christ. Just as there are not many saviors, so are there not many churches founded by Jesus. Because Christ Jesus is the one mediator who offered the once-for-all sacrifice, his body the Church is also one.

The Church's oneness similarly reflects that of the Holy Trinity, from whom she has her origin and after whom she is patterned. In the words of Vatican II: "The highest exemplar and source of this mystery [the Church's oneness] is the unity, in the Trinity of Persons, of one God, the Father and the Son in the Holy Spirit."[10] Just as the three divine persons are united in "one" nature, so must the Church profess one faith and life as one communion of distinct persons.

Visible Unity

The unity of the Church is not just spiritual but sacramental. It has both a visible and an invisible dimension. Catholics believe that it is God's will that we should be united to Christ within this visible community of disciples originating from his will and given shape by the apostles. Although his commission to Peter (cf. Matthew 16:18-19) and institution of the Eucharist at the last supper both clearly point to Jesus' founding a community that was to survive after his death, it is better to say that the Church is "the fruit of the life of Jesus."[11] Not only does the Church have her historical origin in Christ, it is he who continues to nourish her as his body and send her the Holy Spirit.

The New Testament portrays this early apostolic community as possessing "one heart and one soul" (Acts 2:42, cf. 4:32). Not just sharing a sentimental attachment to the Lord, the first Christians were profoundly aware of being brought together in unity by the Holy Spirit. This unity of heart and mind expressed itself in their adherence to the apostles' preaching. To be a believer meant to accept the apostolic preaching as normative. They shared a common confession of faith. St. Paul understood this unity of faith to be so crucial that he excoriated the Galatians for thinking of changing that faith in even the smallest way: "As we have said before, so now I repeat, if anyone proclaims to you a gospel contrary to what you received, let that one be accursed!" (Galatians 1:9).

The apostolic community likewise broke the one Eucharistic bread together. Already in communion with Christ and with one another, they expressed their common faith in this act of worship, recognizing and celebrating their oneness by sharing the Eucharist. This sacrament both manifested and deepened their unity with one another and with God: “Because there is one bread, we who are many are one body, for we all partake of the one bread” (1 Corinthians 10:17).

Down through the centuries God has preserved this visible unity among those united in confessing the one faith, in celebrating the sacraments, especially the Eucharist, and in recognizing the pastoral authority of the bishops and the Pope.[12] Since the Church is a visible institution or sacrament, it has a tangible unity. Christ has entrusted the bishops, the successors to the apostles, with ensuring her unity in faith and communion. In a special way, the Pope is the center of the Church’s unity.

One principal reason for the great appeal of the Catholic Church is her institutional solidity. She can be identified by her teachings, structures, and law. Because she is so visible, the Church attracts attention. It is of her nature to be seen and heard. Although her inner heart is the hidden life of grace, the visible and invisible (the exterior and the interior) cannot be played off against each other. As in all sacraments, which are visible embodiments of God’s invisible grace, so is the Church herself “one interlocked reality” — a spiritual community and a visible organization. Such concreteness is very comforting. Not elusive, I can find the Church, enter her, and love her.

What Is Special About the Catholic Church?

Christians of nearly every denomination accept that Christ willed and prayed “that there be one visible Church of God.”[13] They disagree, however, about the essential elements of this one Church. Protestants, for example, accept the necessity of baptism but not of sacramental confession. The Orthodox accept all the sacraments but do not recognize the fullness of papal authority.

Although these Churches and ecclesial communities have preserved much of the apostolic faith and even, in some cases such as the Orthodox and Old Catholics, apostolic succession in the ministry, there are not three or more equal branches of the one Church. Christ's Church is not just "a collection — divided, but still possessing a certain unity — of churches and ecclesial communities."[14] This so-called "branch theory" gives no unique place to the Catholic Church. Its vision of unity could be compared to an agreement among the Big Three automakers in Detroit, each of which is a partner in the automotive industry.

The Catholic claim is straightforward. At Vatican II the bishops taught that the Catholic Church expresses fully, though not exclusively, the visible communion of believers that God desires: "For it is through Christ's Catholic Church alone, which is the all-embracing means of salvation, that the fullness of the means of salvation can be obtained."[15] Only in the Catholic Church is the *fullness* of ecclesial life willed by Christ found.

Non-Catholics often mistake this claim for its supposed arrogance. Yet it simply acknowledges that God has preserved the unity of his Church. Notice that the council spoke of possessing the fullness of the "*means* of salvation." It recognized that the Catholic Church is "institutionally perfect" but did not assert that Catholics are necessarily more grace-filled. Indeed "many elements of sanctification and truth are found outside her visible confines."[16] The Fathers deliberately left open the possibility that non-Catholics could live the mystery of divine grace more profoundly than Catholics. In other words, Catholics cannot claim to be holier than others simply because they belong to the Catholic Church.

Nor is this full Church, already present in the world, merely a future reality to be awaited in hope, a goal that all denominations must strive to reach. No — the fullness of the Church is even now here! Catholics accept that Christ's Church — full and therefore "true" — already exists.

What About the Others?

The Catholic Church then is not just one church among many. She is the single source from which all others have, at some time and in one way or another, separated themselves. Such splits among Christians have been painful ruptures, with guilt on both sides.[17] Fortunately these divisions have also been partial, so that the restoration of full visible unity has a solid foundation to build on.

Until not too long ago, many Catholics embraced an "all or nothing" approach to the Church. Only two choices were available: You belonged either to the "true" (that is, Catholic) Church or to a "false" (or non-Catholic) church. As "false," such self-professed churches were not in themselves thought to be instruments of grace for their adherents. Saving grace was assuredly present in individual Christian believers *despite* their belonging to such churches or communities. What they received from their membership in such bodies was a set of errors that divided them from the true Church.

One great blessing of Vatican II is its teaching that the Catholic Church is *not* the only "true" church founded by Christ. In other churches and ecclesial communities, the Gospel is preached, sacraments are celebrated, and Christian virtue is practiced. To call them "false" churches does not do justice to what the Fathers of the Council taught: "Moreover, some, even very many, of the most significant elements and endowments that together go to build up and give life to the Church itself, can exist outside the visible boundaries of the Catholic Church: the written word of God; the life of grace; faith, hope and charity, with the other interior gifts of the Holy Spirit, as well as visible elements."[18]

The Catholic Church might not be the only "true" church, but in her teaching, sacraments, and ministry she is the fullest manifestation now present in the world of God's plan to bring his people into one. She gratefully acknowledges that "many elements of sanctification and of truth" are found outside her visible structure and considers these "as gifts belonging to the Church of Christ, . . . forces impelling toward catholic unity."[19]

They belong, so to speak, "by right to the one Church of Christ."[20] Because of what is already shared (the Scriptures, baptism, and many fundamental Christian doctrines), true links exist between the Catholic Church and the other churches — bonds of *imperfect communion.* In the words of Vatican II: Those "who believe in Christ and have been properly baptized are put in some, though imperfect, communion with the Catholic Church."[21]

These bonds are called imperfect, since in each non-Catholic church or community at least one essential element is lacking. In the Catholic Church, by divine providence, no such element is lacking; all Catholics are united by the visible bonds of professing the same faith, celebrating the same sacraments, and recognizing the authority of the bishops and Pope.[22] Whereas the goal of ecumenism is to restore full communion among all Christian churches and communities with the Catholic Church, such communion already truly exists among the particular churches (dioceses) united with the bishop of Rome.

Who Is Obliged to Belong to the Church?

Thos have been attracted by Catholic life and doctrine must at some point decide whether to join the Catholic Church. This decision is among life's most serious. Although the traditional adage "Outside the Church there is no salvation"[23] has sometimes been unwisely used to browbeat non-Catholics into the Church, it nonetheless contains a truth that deserves our attention. Indeed, it highlights the fact that belonging to the Church is not optional but necessary.[24]

In their desire to emphasize the Church's importance, especially when dealing with those tempted to separate themselves from her, some early Fathers made strong statements open to misinterpretation. In the third century, St. Cyprian declared that "to be able to have God as Father, it is necessary to have the Church as Mother."[25] And at the beginning of the fifth century,

St. Augustine wrote that "outside the Catholic Church you can find everything except salvation."[26] Such texts could be multiplied.

To interpret these Fathers correctly we must carefully distinguish between the absolute necessity of the Church for salvation and the obligation of individuals to belong to her. All salvation is through Jesus, whether an individual knows it or not; Jesus works in the world through his Church. If the Fathers' statements are to be applied to individuals, then I think that each should be conditioned by the phrase "If you know the Church to be true and have been called to belong to her, then. . ." That is, belonging to the Church is absolutely necessary for those who have seen the light and receive the call.

What these rigorist views of the Church's necessity conveyed was the urgency and seriousness of belonging to her. Christ and his body the Church were the chosen instruments of salvation. These facts are indisputable. They follow from Peter's confession before the Sanhedrin: "There is salvation in no one else, for there is no other name under heaven given among mortals by which we must be saved" (Acts 4:12). Unfortunately not all Catholics made sufficiently clear the difference between every individual's need for Christ as Savior and full Church membership. It is essential to hold the absolute necessity of the former but only the relative necessity of the latter.

In the 1940s, when Father Leonard Feeney of Boston insisted that the ancient maxim "Outside the Church, there is no salvation" meant that only (Roman) Catholics could be saved, Rome declared his views heretical. The Holy Office, without in any way compromising Christ's teaching, clarified that "it is not always required [for salvation] that a person be incorporated in reality as a member of the Church."[27] Everyone had to be related to the Church by desire, but this did not have to be explicit. In some mysterious way, therefore, all those who are saved are linked to the Church. At Vatican II, the Fathers said: "To this catholic unity of the people of God, therefore, . . . all are called, and they belong to it or are ordered to it in various ways, whether they be Catholic faithful or others who believe in Christ or finally all people everywhere who by the grace of God are called to salvation."[28]

Even though *I* must belong to the Catholic Church in order to be saved, since my conscience would allow no other choice, the same cannot automatically be said of everyone. "God . . . desires everyone to be saved" (1 Timothy 2:4), and his divine saving will is not confined to those who belong to the Catholic Church. The Second Vatican Council stated clearly that "those can also attain to everlasting salvation who through no fault of their own do not know the Gospel of Christ or his Church, yet sincerely seek God and, moved by grace, strive by their deeds to do his will as it is known to them through the dictates of conscience."[29] Christ died for everyone. Since the ultimate calling to each of us comes from God and is therefore universal, Catholics believe "that the Holy Spirit offers everyone the possibility of sharing in this Paschal Mystery in a manner known only to God."[30] In God's plan, all salvation comes through Jesus, the "one mediator between God and humankind" (1 Timothy 2:5), although people might be unaware that Christ's saving grace is the cause of their salvation.

Catholics then accept two truths. First, the real possibility of salvation exists for all humanity. "Basing itself upon Sacred Scripture and Tradition, it [Vatican II] teaches that the Church, now sojourning on earth as an exile, is necessary for salvation."[31] Second, all salvation is through Christ, the only one through whom we come to the Father, and his covenanted bride, the Church, with whom he is indissolubly united.[32]

Before the Second Vatican Council, Henri de Lubac prophetically restated the traditional axiom relating to salvation and the Church: "Not 'outside the Church you are damned; but it is by the Church and by the Church alone that you will be saved.' For it is through the Church that salvation will come, that it is already coming to mankind."[33] In the Church's Third Eucharistic Prayer, the celebrant prays that the sacrifice that has made our peace with God may "advance the peace and salvation of all the world." The grace of the Church's Eucharist flows like a river refreshing all humanity.

Gift of Fullness

If God's saving power is effective outside the Catholic Church, a person might rightly ask, "Why then become a Catholic?" Using a cost-benefit analysis approach, such an individual might falsely conclude that no "saving" advantage comes from being Catholic. Without questioning that the Holy Spirit is like the wind that "blows where it chooses" (John 3:8), even outside the Catholic Church's visible boundaries, it remains true that she alone offers the *fullness* of revealed truth that God wants us to know so that we will love him more deeply and celebrate his merciful grace in the Church.

The British apologist and writer C. S. Lewis once said that the only reason for believing anything is that it is true. If you don't think it's true, then don't believe it. This means that if you doubt that the Catholic Church bears authentic witness to Christ in her dogmas, moral teachings, and sacraments, then you are not yet ready to belong to her. No matter how cozy the community or pleasing the liturgy, if you do not believe the Catholic Church originates with Christ and has the fullness of the means of salvation, then you are unprepared to embrace her.

Where does this leave the honest inquirer? If you come to believe what the Church teaches, including her understanding that Christ chose her as his instrument of salvation, then you have a strict obligation to become Catholic. Failure to enter the Church would seriously imperil your salvation.[34] For those called, entry into the Catholic Church is not an option but an obligation — the most wonderful gift imaginable.

Our Holy Home

"HOLY MOTHER CHURCH." THAT'S WHAT CATHOLICS OF A GENERATION ago frequently called the people of God. Unfortunately this once-familiar designation has fallen into disuse. Maybe the maternal image is too sentimental. Perhaps it's not "politically correct" in an age that studiously avoids all gender references in religious discourse. Or, perhaps, it's more flattering to think of ourselves as independent adults than as children with a mother. Whatever the reason, we're missing something when we ignore the Church's femininity, her motherhood. Being a Catholic involves you with a great family. Belonging to the Church means having a mother, beautiful, tender, and lending her hand to sinner and saint alike.

Although holy, the Church scandalizes us with her humanity. She is a refuge for sinners. Inserted into history, she walks our way — a pilgrimage laden with sin as well as glory. Being both human and divine the Church constantly provokes saint and sinner alike. Yet it is *this* Church that I love.

The Church's Femininity

According to many Church Fathers, the Church was born from the pierced side, the wound, of the dying New Adam on the cross, just as Eve was born from sleeping Adam's side (cf. Genesis 2:22-23).[1] From Christ's sleep of death, the Church — the New Eve and true mother of the living (cf. Genesis 3:20) — was born.

The Catholic Church celebrates her femininity and maternity by singing the praises of the Virgin Mary. Her liturgy, especially in the yearly cycle of feasts dedicated to Mary, recalls the joys and sorrows of motherhood. Unabashedly the Church manifests her tenderness by observing conceptions, births, the visit of pregnant women, a lost child, and worried parents — all events associated with a mother's life. Though the Scriptures give remarkably little space to the infancy narratives (only two chapters each in St. Matthew and St. Luke), popular piety, reflected in religious art, has guaranteed the place of motherhood in Catholic devotion and theology.

To call the Church "Mother" draws attention to her profound relationship both with Christ and with us. If stripped of her femininity, the Church would be in danger of being reduced to a purely sociological entity, a multinational corporation with Roman headquarters. Were this to happen, then she would truly be the patriarchal institution so reviled by radical feminists.

Church as Bride

In the Old Testament, the relation of God to his people is often compared to a marriage bond.[2] The Lord God is portrayed as the "husband" of Israel, his bride (cf. Hosea 1—3). Isaiah the prophet wrote lyrically of the chosen people: "For your maker is your husband, the LORD of hosts is his name" (Isaiah 54:5). This metaphor is surprising, given Israel's forceful rejection of fertility cults and sacred marriages between the gods. What the sacred authors wanted to convey was God's relationship of intimacy and companionship with his people. He loved Israel as a husband loves his wife. This communion between partners was not a business transaction regulated by rules, but a covenant. Despite Israel's innumerable infidelities, her chasing after foreign gods, the Lord God healed his fallen spouse through his own unswerving fidelity. For God the covenant is a lasting commitment, and "he remains faithful to his spousal love even if the bride often shows herself to be unfaithful."[3]

Drawing upon this tradition, Jesus described himself as a "bridegroom" in explaining why his disciples did not fast (cf. Mark 2:19). John the Baptist depicted himself as the "best man" waiting for the groom (cf. John 3:29), who was Christ. Though the Scriptures do not explicitly identify the bride, she is undoubtedly the community for whom Christ would shed his blood.

Following Jesus' lead, St. Paul described his own activity as that of the spiritual father of the Corinthians. By preaching to them the Gospel, he was preparing his spiritual daughter, the Christian community in Corinth, for her wedding with Christ. He wrote: "I promise you in marriage to one husband, to present you as a chaste virgin to Christ" (2 Corinthians 11:2).

Later, the apostle Paul, in describing the intimate love-relationship between Christ and his bride, wrote that "Christ loved the Church and gave himself up for her in order to make her holy" (Ephesians 5:25-26). Like the faithful God revealed in the Old Testament, so was Christ faithful in the same way. The Church is the bride, the woman loved who is to become "one flesh" with Jesus, her bridegroom (cf. Ephesians 5:31). She is a collective subject, a community, the people of God. At the same time, Christ loves each individual, each member of his body.[4] As bridegroom, Jesus has entered history and given himself to us in the most radical way: "No one has greater love than this" (John 15:13). He has made us all his bride as the fruit of his love.

The Bible portrays Christ's final triumph over the forces of evil as a great wedding (cf. Revelation 19:7). At the end of time, Christ will come from heaven to meet his bride and unite her totally with himself. Then the promised virgin will become his wife. Not until the Church reaches her fulfillment in the glory of heaven will she cease to carry the mark of this passing world.[5]

This bridal femininity of the Church discloses to us some important truths. As bride, the Church remains distinct from her groom. Despite their oneness, the Church is never simply absorbed or overwhelmed by Christ. Her own identity is preserved — as is that of each of us when we are united to Christ in the Church. That is why today's Church is also the Church of sinners. Christ will always be faithful to his people. Even though their individual fidelity is far from guaranteed, Christ will never divorce his Church. The "one flesh" of the union between bride and groom is a permanent covenant.

Even more important, the bridal imagery helps us to understand that the Church "is subject to Christ" (Ephesians 5:24). Clearly it is the Lord's Church — not one of our own making. Any tendency to compromise Christ's sovereignty over the Church is bound to fail. Triumphalism, grasping for power, and authoritarianism — all of these contradict her inner life. The minute we imagine that the Church could pass into merely human hands, then she would be less than the reality willed and loved by the Lord himself.

So many problems arise when people think of the Church as "theirs." No, she is *his* Church, because she is his bride. If the Church were just another human institution, a free association of those who believed in Jesus' message, then her structure and her teaching could be radically changed. Quite simply, such a Church would be the work of human hands — and ours to mold according to whatever needs seemed most pressing at the time. As Christ's bride she is never to be treated as if she could be changed merely because she is old or held by some to be irrelevant.

Church as Mother

Overshadowed by the Holy Spirit who continues his life-giving activity in her, the Church becomes our mother in baptism: "By her preaching she brings forth to a new and immortal life the sons and daughters who are born to her in baptism, conceived of the Holy Spirit and born of God."[6] In the ancient Church, the pools that the catechumens stepped into for the sacred rite of baptism were frequently shaped like a womb. By entering the Church, they acquired a new mother. A fourth-century instruction for catechumens preparing for baptism admonished them: "Hurry to your mother. . . . Enter, be happy. You are soon going to be nursed, joyously, all together."[7] Going down into the waters the catechumens, now vested in white robes, emerged "born of water and Spirit" (John 3:5). The Church brings forth this new life for Christ by baptism. Through her fruitfulness she gives the Lord his children of whom she is the mother. In the third century, St. Cyprian summed up the connection between the Church's maternity and adopted sonship when he wrote that "he alone can have God as his Father who first has the Church as his mother!"[8]

The Church is not just a mother in giving birth but also in the difficult task of forming her offspring. In ordinary mother-child relations, the child is eventually weaned away from his or her mother. When Mother Church gives birth to her children in baptism, however, she does not separate them from her body. She accepts them into her. No separation from the Church's protective guardianship over her children ever takes place. Mother and child remain linked. The Church's maternal role continues throughout life, nurturing us with her "milk" of preaching, teaching, sacraments, and Eucharist. Like the disciples who gathered around Jesus and formed with him permanent bonds of friendship — and unlike a school from which we eventually graduate! — so also are the baptized abidingly tied to the Church.

Church as Family

According to Genesis, our creation in God's image and likeness is a call to community. "It is not good that the man should be alone" (Genesis 2:18). The vocation to love necessarily involves us with others. As Adam became fully alive only in communion with God *and Eve*, so God calls us to communion with others in his Church.

With the Church as our mother, we are all children in the same great family. In this communion of saints, everyone is to bear the other's burdens and share the other's joys. We beg the saints to intercede for us. We pray for those in purgatory. We are bound by ties of charity and justice to all the brethren.

As in all families, we are linked to our brothers and sisters. "All the saints and the angels belong to us," wrote Henri de Lubac; "the heroism of the missionary, the inspiration of the doctors of the Church, the generosity of the martyrs, the genius of the artists, the burning prayer of the Carmelites — it is as if all that were ourselves; it is ourselves."[9] Not even death destroys our bonds with all those who are "called children of God" (1 John 3:1). Mother Church is wide open — through time, space, and history.

Not a small group of like-minded individuals, she is a universal Church that draws her children from every tribe and tongue and people and nation (cf. Revelation 5:9). As a family of disciples, the Church's vision spans the centuries. Not elitist, she has room for every culture, class, educational level, and personal temperament. This family is as wide as the world.

The Church is humanity's natural home. That's why so many converts speak spontaneously of "coming home" when describing their entry into the Church. Securely enfolded in the arms of Mother Church, Catholics are not, in Walker Percy's phrase, "lost in the cosmos." They are at home. They know where they are going and how to get there. And they have a gentle hand to guide them. That's what mothers do.

Holy Church of Sinners

Yet the Church is holy. Not on her own, but because Christ "gave himself up for her, in order to make her holy by cleansing her with the washing of water by the word, so as to present the church to himself in splendor, without a spot or wrinkle or anything of the kind — yes, so that she may be holy and without blemish" (Ephesians 5:25-27).[10] By loving her he has made her lovable. Not an institution founded in the past and then launched on its own into history, the Church is the constant recipient of Christ's spousal love. Because I am in the Church, I too am loved.

In the Old Testament, the people of God was holy because it was chosen by God: "If you obey my voice and keep my covenant, you shall be my treasured possession out of all the peoples" (Exodus 19:6, cf. 24:4-8). Likewise, in the New Testament the Church is described as the people of God, a "holy nation" (1 Peter 2:9) and a "holy temple" (Ephesians 2:21). It is God himself who sets her apart and marks her as his own. Holiness resides in the Church because of Christ's presence in her and his sending of the Spirit as the giver of life. Because of her divine election, the Church has received this God-given "objective" holiness as a gift.

United to Christ, the Church is both sanctified and sanctifies.[11] She is "an instrument for the redemption of all, and is sent forth into the whole world as the light of the world and the salt of the earth."[12] The Church manifests her sanctifying power primarily through celebrating the sacraments.

Catholic belief in "holy Church" would be frightening, even off-putting, if it were not accompanied by an equally insistent teaching that the Church is for us sinners.[13] The same St. Paul who plumbed the mystery of the Church "in splendor" also wrote that "God proves his love for us in that while we were still sinners Christ died for us" (Romans 5:8). Through the centuries she has consistently repudiated the attempts of those who wanted to exclude sinful members from the Church, limiting her to being a sect only for the sinless and the elect. St. John's reprimand that "if we have no sin in us we deceive ourselves" (1 John 1:8) is asserted not only out of humility but because it is true. We do not need the media's pillorying and readiness to uncover scandals in the Church to be aware that she embraces sinners. To be honest, most of us need to look no farther than in the mirror. The Second Vatican Council restated the belief that the holiness of the Church did not exclude sinners: "The Church, embracing in its bosom sinners, at the same time holy and always in need of being purified, always follows the way of penance and renewal."[14] If the Church's holiness were already perfectly realized in all her members, then she would need neither purification nor renewal![15]

Because Christians continue to sin and seek conversion, we can speak of a "Church of sinners." The designation clarifies the point that insofar as the Church has not yet reached her full glory in heaven, she still embraces this world and the sinners who live within her. Yet we do not speak of a "sinful Church." This could too easily suggest that holiness and sinfulness are on an equal par. That is not true. God has clothed his bride with a holiness that comes from him and not from us.

The really good news is that our sins cannot destroy the presence of Christ in the Church. As a "foreign" element that tarnishes her, sin is always subordinate to holiness. Their relationship can best be summed up by the phrase "holy Church of sinners."

Yet if the Church is holy, this should be discernible. At the First Vatican Council the Fathers rather grandiloquently proclaimed that the "eminent holiness" of the Church is itself "a great and perpetual motive of credibility and an irrefutable testimony of her divine mission."[16] How does the Church honestly measure up to this?

Besides the holiness coming from her divine origin, some visible signs also disclose her interior life. The witness of holy lives, especially of the saints, is among the most compelling reasons for affirming the Church's holiness.[17] Their holiness shares in Christ's grace. We meet Christ in them and through them, since he has transformed them into his new creation (cf. 2 Corinthians 5:17). Nor do I mean just the recognized saints whom the Church has canonized so that we may seek their intercession and imitate their example. All who live in grace are "participants of the divine nature" (2 Peter 1:4). Not celebrated publicly, countless millions of men and women throughout the world are saints, made holy by their communion with God. These public and hidden saints embody Christian holiness, constantly reminding us that life in the Church brings such greatness, a greatness that is the vocation of every person washed in the waters of baptism.

The Church's holiness also manifests itself in her being a moral and spiritual leaven in this suffering world. Despite her faults, sometimes caused by excessive zeal, she has inspired civilization with the highest ideals of justice, peace, sexual fidelity, concern for the poor, respect for life — and others too numerous to mention.

A sign of the majesty of the Church's holiness is her ongoing mission of welcoming sinners into her bosom. This is the greatest scandal of all for those who think the Church is only for the saints and turn away from her because she embraces public sinners. How many critics unearth the unholy actions of certain popes and prelates as an argument against the Church! And how many people say they don't go to church because "they're all hypocrites." Both miss the point of Christ's redeeming love. It is a gift to us who fail.

No one who is truly contrite is ever excluded from her sacraments. The Church's mercy, like her Lord's, is boundless. I think she is never more holy than when ministering to sinners. Never condemning the sinner, whom she wants to be converted, she fights against sin. Like St. Paul, the Church endlessly entreats us to "be reconciled to God" (2 Corinthians 5:20).

Church as Home

The more we appreciate the beauty of the Church, her closeness to Christ and her exalted calling, the more we are hurt by her setbacks and the more we are saddened by her less-than-perfect holiness. Belonging to the Church inevitably brings disappointments with it. When inquirers express an interest in Catholicism, I have sometimes tried, quite mistakenly, to shield them from its seamier side, lacking confidence that they could see beyond it. This is not so different from the instinctive shield we often put up for family problems. You don't wash your dirty laundry in public. If such a protective guard could be raised in the past, for better or for worse it can't be any longer. The sexual escapades of clerics, Vatican financial malfeasance, and seemingly endless internal squabbling and name-calling have all been found newsworthy. The laundry hamper of scandals has been emptied and displayed for all to see.

Yet, despite these assaults, the Church remains our holy mother, our home, and our family. In human families, as children grow older they discover, often to their great dismay, their mother's weaknesses. Let down, they are prone to make harsh judgments about her and are tempted to tell her what she should do. Complaining about their mother's faults, they measure her virtue against their expectations of ideal motherhood.

Similarly, how easy it is for the Church's children to whine, "Does the Church meet *my* expectations?" It is all too easy for us to gripe about her. Sometimes, because we are disappointed, we raise our voices against the Church — as if she were other than ourselves. But I am a Christian, a Catholic, only in her and never apart from her. Mature children do not stand at a critical distance from their mother complaining about her faults. Despite her shortcomings, they are willing to support her in her weakness.

On this score Hans Urs von Balthasar recalls the humility of the saints, pointing out that they remain childlike toward the Church. The mediocrity of her members and institutions does not deter them from fully identifying with her. Why? They know "well enough that without the Church they would not find their way to God." Disillusion does not lead them away from their mother. Saints, even when they suffer at the hands of fellow Catholics, never become resentful. Nor do they "stand sulkily aside."[18] They do not attempt to get on good terms with God on their own initiative, leaving Christ's Church aside and forming a community apart.

If you are ever tempted to criticize the Church with a bitter heart, recall how isolated you would be without her. Precisely because the Church is incarnate, tangible, and visible in her teaching and her sacraments, no effort is needed to uncover her faults. It would be so easy to escape into a misty and disembodied Church judged to be "perfect." But that would not be the body Christ founded.

We must take the Church as she is given to us in the concrete. To belong to the Church means to abandon our own idea of her and throw in our lot with this group of people, with this parish, with these teachings, with this bishop, and with this Pope. At times we might be scandalized or disillusioned because the Church is moving too fast or too slow, is too rich or too poor, too progressive or too reactionary. Yet we must learn, as St. Ignatius Loyola insisted, to live, think, and feel with the Church as she is. This is the mother whom the Lord has given us, the Church to which we belong.

Because the Church has a human side, she is cause for scandal, even hatred. Undoubtedly her sinful members have abused her splendor through the centuries. If she were disembodied, rather than immersed in the world, she would escape such criticism. Were she to mind her own spiritual business in the sacristy, she would be tolerated. In neither case, however, would the Church be faithful to her divine mission.

Behind this antipathy to the visible Church is a judgment at odds with Catholic piety. A falsely "spiritualizing" view is now present in our culture. It is a worldview that masks itself as refined piety, looking down its nose at a Catholicism cluttered with statues, saints, and sacraments. Vilifying institutions, the adherents of this worldview preach escape from the created world. Religious persons, they say, are supposed to transcend the material. These "new age" ideas have unfortunately spilled over even into the Church. You can easily recognize them in the harangues ridiculing the institutional Church. Such critics want a privatized faith freed from the all-too-visible body of the Church.

All such attempts to separate the Church as an "institution" from the Spirit of the risen Lord — who enlivens her — fall into a pernicious dualism. We Catholics are earthy people celebrating our faith in God's Son who has entered our history, married the Church, and remains among us. More than ever we must emphasize that the Word made flesh is the central mystery of our faith. He covenanted humanity through his incarnation and redemption, saving us through his visible Church and feeding us with his real flesh and blood in the Eucharist.

Because God calls us through his Son's visible body, every Catholic has an ecclesial vocation. To be a disciple is to follow him in his body, the Church. Catholics do not deny that God can communicate directly with his creation — he does — but the privileged way *he* chose for such interaction was his Church. Because Christ and the Church are "one flesh," the eyes of the believer behold the face of Christ in this Church. Christ and the Church are indissolubly united. Here Christ is alive! Here Christ is loved!

If the Church were merely a human institution, without a divine heart, it would be idolatry to love her. But the so-called "institution" of the Church — her members, her rites of worship, her teachings — is not simply a shell for Christ that we can discard at will. The head of the Church does not save his people without his body. The Church mediates our encounter with Christ.

In a world that preaches that we should always keep our options open, Catholics are a breed apart. We take a stand. We throw in our lot with the visible Church. We take her for better or for worse. “Just as Christ loved the church and gave himself up for her” (Ephesians 5:25), so we also must become lovers of the Church. If we linger on the fringes as neutral observers, we shall never grasp her depth. Only a lover can draw near to the core of her mystery. Only those who love can understand and dare to criticize.

The Church deserves our love because she is worthy of Christ’s love as the bride whom he has purified and made glorious. She is the home to which all are called and where all are loved. Already, in the second century, St. Irenaeus put it very plainly: “In the measure that one loves the Church of Christ, one possesses the Holy Spirit.” Without this burning love it makes no sense to belong to the Church.

Bodily Vision

AS A HISTORICAL RELIGION, CATHOLICISM IS ROOTED IN THE FOUNDATIONAL events of Jesus' birth, ministry, death, and resurrection. We accept the testimony of those who heard, looked at, and even touched Jesus, the Word of life (cf. 1 John 1:1). Because Jesus thought with a human mind, worked with human hands, and loved with a human heart, God is no outsider to humanity. Catholics take seriously this mystery of the incarnation, the Son's living the adventure of human life among us. The *Catechism of the Catholic Church* speaks of the incarnation as *the* distinctive sign of Christian faith.[1]

"Enfleshment" of God's Son

What is the incarnation? The English term comes from the Latin *incarnatio*, which means "enfleshing." The incarnation is the "enfleshment" of God's eternal Son in the womb of the Nazarene Virgin. First proclaimed by Peter on a dusty road at Caesarea Philippi, the Church's unshakable faith is that Jesus is "the Son of the living God" (Matthew 16:16). After the resurrection, the apostle Thomas cried out, "My Lord and my God!" (John 20:28) when Jesus invited him to place his hands in his wounds. And St. John began his Gospel with that awesome text: "In the beginning was the Word, and the Word was with God and the Word was God. . . . And the Word became flesh and lived among us" (John 1:1, 14). At the heart of our faith is the joyful proclamation "that Jesus Christ has come in the flesh" (1 John 4:2). We do not know what it means to be divine, but Catholics believe that to whatever small degree this mystery can be plummeted they can say no less of Jesus than what the Nicene Creed confesses: He is "true God from true God."

What made Jesus so immediately attractive to his followers

was, however, his humanity: born in a stable, lost in the temple, tempted in the desert, angry with the money changers, and tortured on the cross. Flesh of our flesh, Jesus had a body and soul like ours. The Church has steadfastly maintained that the riches of his humanity in no wise minimize his divinity. There is nothing second-rate or remote about Jesus' manhood, he who "had to become like his brothers and sisters in every respect, so that he might be a merciful and faithful high priest in the service of God" (Hebrews 2:17). He was indeed a man like us in all things but sin (cf. Hebrews 4:15). Jesus was truly, indeed *fully*, human. We are less than fully human because we diminish our humanity by sin in a way that Jesus did not. Saints after all are more human, not less human, than sinners!

Yet the mystery and fascination of Jesus — and ultimately the reason for his lasting impact on us — is that he was and is both true God *and* true man. "Though he was in the form of God . . . he emptied himself, taking the form of a slave, being born in human likeness" (Philippians 2:6, 7). He alone of all creatures unites the divine and the human; he alone bridges the chasm between the uncreated and the created, between heaven and earth.

One thing Catholics know for sure about this mystery, and the Church tirelessly repeats: We do not make Jesus more "accessible" to modern people by diminishing his divinity. Exalting his humanity, his life among us and for us, should not lead to obscuring that "in him all the fullness of God was pleased to dwell" (Colossians 1:19). The staunch faith of the Church, the ultimate preserver of his mesmerizing mystery,[2] is that the One who comes to us as true God, as the very Son of the Father, also comes as one like us, who "in the days of his flesh . . . offered up prayers and supplications, with loud cries and tears" to his Father (Hebrews 5:7). This is the source of the fascination. What was almost "incredible" to Jews and Greeks alike was that a man such as Jesus — who was born of a woman, got tired and hungry, wept at his friend's death, and was crucified like a criminal — should be God. The Church confesses nothing less.

The incarnation, which emphasizes the *bodily* coming of God's Son into the world, leaves its seal on every aspect of Catholic life. In praise of the Church's bodily-incarnational vision, Christopher Derrick writes: "The Catholic Faith is an incarnational, even a carnal, thing: I have heard it described as the sexiest of all religions. The uniting of flesh and blood with the supremely Sacred lies at the heart of its belief and its worship too, and a bodily and even sexual emphasis recurs constantly in its self-expression."[3] Belonging to the Catholic Church means taking this "enfleshment" seriously in worship and in living.

How the Church worships tells us what she believes. That's why Church authorities so carefully regulate her liturgy, or public prayer. Belonging to the Church steeps us in the Catholic vision of worship: of sacred and immaculate hearts, of the real body of Jesus, of holy oil smeared and hands blessed. As a Catholic you will hear rosaries clatter, see heads bowed, touch relics of saints' bones, smell incense — and perhaps be appalled at exuberant devotions, of bloody statues, and wailing processions. These displays of popular piety, whatever aesthetic failings they may have, remind us of the staggering truth that the Son of God became man and that nothing human is foreign to him.

The Good Creation

I am grateful that the Church's teaching on the incarnation prevents me from succumbing to the temptation of adopting a falsely "spiritual" religious vision. Ironically, our health-conscious and sex-sated society tries to convince us that material creation is insignificant in God's saving plan. It seems to suggest that we ought to aspire to angelic life, the ephemeral world of disembodied spirits where we can live in peace! The Church, however, corrects this seductive view masking itself as piety.

What Americans need is not a more "spiritual" religion but a more incarnational, more sacramental — even more bodily — Christianity. Belonging to the Catholic Church provides this for us. Hilaire Belloc exuberantly expressed Catholicism's world-affirming qualities in a clever ditty:

When'er the Catholic son doth shine,
there's music and laughter and good red wine.
At least I've always found it so—
Benedicamus Domino!

Contrary to those who belittle the material — the flesh of the world — Catholics are unrelenting realists. They take the Lord at his word. As a material and spiritual unity, his creation is "very good" (Genesis 1:31). Whatever Adam and Eve lost in the original Fall, Christ has even more wonderfully restored: "If, because of the one man's trespass, death exercised dominion through that one, much more surely will those who receive the abundance of grace and the free gift of righteousness exercise dominion in life through the one man, Jesus Christ" (Romans 5:17). Theirs was the "happy fault" of which we sing in the Easter Exultet: "O happy fault, O necessary sin of Adam, which gained for us so great a Redeemer!" When the Son took flesh in Mary's womb, he assumed our humanity as an instrument of the divine. Because of the incarnation, says John Paul II, the body has entered "through the main door" of our theology and of our faith.[4]

One of Catholicism's great insights is its insistence that our way to God passes through his creation. Because of Christ, the earth has become God's dwelling place. He uses the created world to mediate his saving grace to us. God "speaks" to us through his creation, which allows human intelligence to "hear" the words of the Creator (cf. Romans 1:19-20).[5] "Man's Maker was made man," wrote St. Augustine, "that he, Ruler of the stars, might nurse at his mother's breasts; that the Bread might be hungry, the Fountain thirst, the Light sleep, the Way be tired from the journey."[6]

Throughout history the incarnation, especially its outcome of obedience to the death of gallows crucifixion, has been a stumbling block for "spiritual" people. St. Paul recognized the shock, even the disdain, the Galilean criminal's claim to be the Son of God provoked: "But we proclaim Christ crucified, a stumbling block to Jews and foolishness to the Gentiles" (1 Corinthians 1:23). The spiritual take offense that God has come to rescue us in an earthly and material way. Fringe spiritual movements have tried "to make God more believable by protecting him from the dust of the earth."[7] By so teaching they imperil Christianity's core belief that God has become one with us in Christ so that we might become one again with God.

Arius, for example, the fourth-century monk whose teaching prompted the first ecumenical council at Nicaea in 325, could not really accept the incarnation. He thought that the Father could not share his life with the Son; therefore, the Son was not "true God from true God." Too grand, too removed, too solitary to bridge the gap, the Father, he taught, dwells in impenetrable solitude. For Arius, the Son was not fully divine. Arius was defeated at the council, and Christians accepted the word of Jesus at face value: "Whoever has seen me, has seen the Father" (John 14:9).

Spiritualist Heresy

All around us is a new "heresy" — the word comes from the Greek word meaning "selection" — a partial view of the truth about creation. This heresy is not readily identifiable with a group that opposes orthodox Christianity. Other than many of the New Age sects, it has no institutional home, no authorities who give it their own name. Yet I think this heresy of *false spiritualizing* is a grave threat to Christianity. Fortunately the

Church has the necessary resources to combat this insidious influence that presents itself as a piety superior to traditional Catholicism.

Already in the early Church our ancestors confronted the heresy of gnosticism. These gnostics, some of whom claimed to be Christians, believed that salvation did not depend on anything created. They refused to admit that the spiritual and the material, the divine and the human, go together. Characteristic of all gnosticism is a dualism that radically opposes the material to the spiritual.[8] For gnostics, divinity is alien and hostile to the world — though it has tragically fallen into material creation. Because of this tragic fall, a "divine spark" is within people, a spark — we might say the "real me" — that must break out of its earthly confinement. Gnostic salvation is escape from the world. Christian redemption is *salus carnis*, salvation *of* the flesh, *through* the flesh of Jesus' passion, death, and bodily resurrection, and *for* our flesh in the resurrection of the body.

Gnosticism recurs today, not in its original form, but as a view denigrating or bypassing creation as the instrument through which God mediates his saving grace to us. This false spiritualism, so evident now in the New Age movement, is running rampant. How do you recognize it? It finds a home among those who question the incarnation as a real event in the history of humanity, who separate the Church as an "institution" from the Spirit of the risen Lord enlivening her, who ridicule outward sacramental mediation as the means by which God sanctifies us, or who sever body from spirit in human sexuality. These neo-gnostic opinions all share a common idea: they deny the awesome fact that God has truly entered our history, that he has covenanted a people to himself and married his Church.

The Sacramental Principle

In the Catholic vision, the created cosmos does not establish an abyss between God and humanity but is itself a sign of his presence. "Ever since the creation of the world his eternal power and divine nature, invisible though they are, have been understood and seen through the things he has made" (Romans 1:20), through the cosmos. "The whole of creation is one grand book which would suffice to reveal to man the divine wisdom," writes Henri de Lubac, "if sin had not darkened this vision."[9] Since he cannot be heard or seen directly, God relies on created realities, visible means, so that his word may be heard and responded to in faith.

In the Old Testament, access to God was mediated through prophetic words, the saving events in Israel, priesthood, cult, Temple, and Jewish law. In the New Covenant, mediation is not abolished but heightened. Bridges between God and creation must still be built. God's love becomes palpable, humanly visible in Jesus Christ; in him the love, mercy, faithfulness, simplicity, and openness of the Trinity have been revealed. As we sing in the First Christmas Preface: "In him we see our God made visible and so are caught up in the love of the God we cannot see." And all this was accomplished through Christ's *body*, now risen and taken into the new creation, where it remains forever glorified.

The fact itself of the incarnation tells us that the created material cosmos is the chosen means through which God communicates his life to us. What is human and visible can bear the divine. Through the Son's taking flesh, "the terrible and tragic rip in the fabric of Creation is being reknit."[10] The Fall is reversed, and spirit and flesh are brought together again. In God's redemptive hands, created realities can serve as instruments of grace. God's own way of saving us is incarnational and therefore sacramental — necessarily involving humanity's return to him through visible means.

Because of the incarnation, humanity returns to God in a bodily or sacramental way. As the Father touched us bodily in his Son's sacred humanity, he leads us back to himself in the same way. Since the Son of God consecrated our humanity first by assuming it and then by redeeming it through his death and resurrection, we dare not think that we shall be saved by ignoring creation.

Human encounters are mediated through created realities. We see, hear, smell, and touch others in communicating with them. We reveal ourselves and discover others through bodily gestures. It is likewise in our encounters with the Christ, the Word made flesh. Divine life comes to us through the actions and words of the Church, acting in his name and in his person.

Even after the ascension, humanity needed the contact of Christ's saving presence for its redemption. The Church provides us with that prolongation of the incarnation. In her, we meet Christ as the ever-present head of his body. Here believers can "touch" the risen Lord. As our bodies are instruments through which we carry out our work and activity in the world, so too does Christ use the Church as his instrument. In her teaching and her sacraments, she perpetuates Jesus' saving word and actions.

Catholics live in his mystical body, the continuation of his glorified body in our world. "From the side of Christ as he slept the sleep of death upon the cross," wrote the Second Vatican Council Fathers, "there came forth the wondrous sacrament which is the whole Church."[11] Christ has taken the Church to himself as the bride with whom he has become "one flesh." Any effort to split Christ from his body — a Christ without the Church — is, as we have seen, futile. In a living body, the head cannot be separated from its members. The Church is truly "one complex reality which comes together from a human and a divine element" that is at the same time "the mystical body of Christ, the visible society and the spiritual community, the earthly Church and the Church endowed with heavenly riches."[12] Catholic realism delivers us from all false dualism that would vilify the visible Church as a useless appendage to the heavenly.

The Magnificent Seven

Being a Catholic is not just about believing truths. It is about friendship with Christ. "I do not call you servants any longer, because the servant does not know what the master is doing; but I have called you friends, because I have made known to you everything that I have heard from my Father" (John 15:15). Jesus is the center of our lives. He does not tell the disciples that he will show them the way to the Father; he announces that he himself is that path: "I am the way, and the truth, and the life. No one comes to the Father except through me" (John 14:6).

It is not enough to affirm religious truths about Jesus, to be able to talk eloquently and convincingly about him. Belonging to the Church commits a person to following the living Lord Jesus who "became obedient to the point of death — even death on a cross" (Philippians 2:8). The focus of our lives must always be Christ: to follow him and to love him, the God-made-man, who has become a companion to us.

Jesus comes to befriend us, so to speak, in the seven sacraments. Through material realities as ordinary as bread, wine, oil, and bodies, God makes present his love and mercy in the rituals Christ gave to the Church. These actions of Christ, which the Church celebrates "until he comes" (1 Corinthians 11:26), sacred tradition calls the "sacramental economy," or plan of salvation.[13]

Unable to hear or see him with our senses, God uses created realities, visible means, so that we may hear his Word and celebrate his love in faith. From washing a baby with water to spouses making love, each of the seven sacraments proclaims that this world does not separate God from humanity. I am thankful that the Church teaches this liberating truth in which

God's work of creation is complementary and not opposed to redemption.

A physical encounter with Jesus, the only way to the Father, is no longer possible as it was in the Palestine of the first believers. Yet, if certain conditions are met, saving encounters can take place in today's Church. God gives his greatest gifts *through* his creation. Our bodily life is not an obstacle but an instrument of salvation. Christ comes to meet his people in the sacraments. They are his hands that touch us and his words that now resound in our ears. Pope St. Leo the Great describes this straight line from Jesus of Nazareth to the sacraments: "What was visible in Christ has now passed over into the sacraments of the Church."[14]

What I find so wonderful in the sacramental plan of salvation is that God, when he communicates with us, respects our nature and way of acting. He saves us as we are — bodily persons. The sacraments are a "language" that we understand. Which of us does not recognize the purifying power of water, the healing of oil and touch, the refreshment of bread and wine? God has provided us with sacraments so that humanity can enjoy his saving benefits as he created us.

Sacramental "Guarantee"

In religious matters, it's dangerous to talk about "guarantees." Such language could all too easily lead us to think that God is somehow indebted to us if we have purchased the saving goods. The Catholic tradition is adamant in declaring with St. Paul that "by grace you have been saved through faith, and this is not your own doing; it is the gift of God" (Ephesians 2:8). Yet, if we take the new and everlasting covenant seriously, we can count on God's fidelity to his Church. This promise too takes an incarnational form that Catholics emphasize in their sacramental teaching. Deeply rooted in the Catholic tradition is the belief that the seven sacraments "work" because of God's unfailing faithfulness, a faithfulness realized through human actions. How is this so?

Sacraments are *Christ's* own saving actions, carried out through and in the Church. When he acts, he does so mercifully and lovingly; that is, such acts bestow grace on those who celebrate them. Their gratuity is not compromised if we were to say they "contain" this promise of grace. God is not capricious or arbitrary in his offer but steadfast in his love. In a world where religion has become privatized and falls easily under the sway of feeling, it is a relief to know that the grace of the sacraments does not depend upon the interpersonal dynamics between minister and recipient.

Total strangers often meet in the confessional. Whether a good feeling results between priest and penitent is secondary. It is not the priest's "niceness" that forgives sin. It is Christ. As inspiring as it sometimes is to know the priest who is offering the Eucharist, Catholics believe that this personal rapport is not crucial. Christ is the main celebrant.[15]

Catholicism emphasizes the immediacy of Christ's action in the sacraments. That's why the faithful are not beholden to unworthy ministers. If your own dispositions are good, you need never worry whether a sacrament is truly celebrated, provided it is carried out according to the Church's mind and practice.

In the third and fourth centuries, some Christians began to affirm that the holiness of the minister determined sacramental efficacy. The Church's response was unequivocal. Sacraments are not spiritual powers that flow from the minister; rather, they are Christ's actions in his body. No one is clearer than St. Augustine: "What Paul bestowed, what Peter bestowed is Christ's. For the power is Christ's, the administration is the Apostle's. . . . Therefore, anyone baptized by Judas has been baptized by Christ, just as anyone baptized by a drunkard, by a murderer, or by an adulterer has been baptized by Christ."[16]

Whenever a sacrament is rightly celebrated, Catholics are confident that Christ is at work. It is his Church!

"Little" Sacraments: Catholic Devotions

The incarnational-sacramental dimension of Catholicism demands traditions that embody her bodily vision. They speak a language that keeps the Church vital, incarnated in every culture. Worthwhile traditions sustain and transmit essential truths. They lend warmth, familiarity, and security to our living the Gospel. For centuries St. Francis of Assisi's Christmas crib has inspired men and women to ponder the wondrous message of the Word made flesh in the womb of the Virgin Mary. Such a tradition, though not essential, is a powerful commentary on the Creed's confession that "by the power of the Holy Spirit he was born of the Virgin Mary and became man." Without human traditions such as this, the sacramental economy would lack some of the supports that enrich it.

Unfortunately contemporary society is not comfortable with religious ritual and human traditions. Christian worship, they say, is essentially a spiritual activity. Human traditions, with their embarrassing tangibility and emphasis on externals, seem far removed from Jesus' demand for worship "in spirit and truth" (John 4:23). Everything material and bodily — from lighting candles to sprinkling holy water to visiting Fátima — is frowned upon. These gestures are, they maintain, too easy, too external, and too worldly to be taken seriously as authentic religious practices!

In the early years of his pontificate, John Paul II dedicated many of his weekly Wednesday discourses to his "theology of the body." Repeatedly he insisted that the incarnation places the body and material creation at the center of our faith.[17] Most Catholic devotions — like processions, novenas, and wearing blessed medals — are venerable traditions embodying that fundamental Catholic sense that the material cosmos is not evil but the means which God has chosen to share his life with us.

Because of this strongly incarnational perspective, the Catholic tradition has cultivated a sense that human beings should feel "at home in the world."[18] The Church has encouraged innumerable traditions — practices and devotions — that she understands to be extremely helpful in experiencing the world through Catholic eyes and, even more important, with a Catholic heart. Traditions involving the times and seasons have their place in our devotion, since we are beings who live in history. Spaces, places, and special clothing are also indispensable. That's why we build beautiful cathedrals, set aside sanctuary areas, wear religious habits, and buy our children First Communion outfits.

Material objects and blessings fill Catholic life with reminders of the mysteries of creation and redemption. "There is hardly any proper use of material things," declared Vatican II, "which cannot thus be directed toward the sanctification of men and women and the praise of God."[19] The variety of traditions is endless: blessing fields, walking the way of the cross, saying rosaries, venerating crucifixes and statues in churches and homes.

Believers sanctify their everyday life primarily by presenting their bodies "as a living sacrifice, holy and acceptable to God," their "spiritual worship" (Romans 12:1). But they accompany their bodily gift with other visible signs, reminding themselves that God blesses every dimension of their life. These sacred signs allow created realities to reveal the eternal by directing us heavenward, fulfilling St. Paul's advice to set our minds "on things that are above" (Colossians 3:2). They saturate and sanctify human life "with divine energy."[20]

The Church has no definitive list of sacramentals. She multiplies them according to need. In medieval Europe, ecclesiastics threw a net of blessings over every dimension of life: from food to animals, from throats to vines. As the Church moves through history we can look forward to a continual unfolding of new "little sacraments" that will help to restore all things in Christ.

If we acquire a love for these sacramentals we become rich with the collective wealth of the Church's experience, wisdom, and beauty. We should therefore rejoice in her heritage of holiness and devotions, not as a cult of nostalgia to escape into an antiquity that is no longer present but to take pleasure, encouragement, and enlightenment in the saints, the music, the piety of those who have made up the Catholic family over the centuries.

"The whole world is a sacrament," writes Peter Kreeft, "a sacred thing, a gift; and the sacramental character of the world reminds us of the central sacrament, the Incarnation, continued among us in the seven sacraments of the Church, especially in the Eucharist."[21] Through these seven visible signs of invisible and life-giving grace, the human person encounters Christ in his body, the Church. Since we cannot hear or see God directly, we rely on created realities to bring him first to us and us back to him. The Catholic Church lives the incarnational, bodily, and sacramental plan that is just what the Divine Physician ordered.

It's the Mass That Matters

NOTHING IS MORE PRECIOUS TO CATHOLICS THAN THE MASS. OVER the centuries Catholics have been persecuted for going to Mass, martyred for hiding the Eucharist, ridiculed for adoring Jesus' body and blood in transformed bread and wine. They have also written poems and composed music of lasting beauty in praise of Christ's immortal body and walked in innumerable processions holding aloft the Sacred Host as their trophy of victory. When Catholics are baptized, married, and buried, they do so at Mass.

The Eucharist is central to Catholic identity. This most awesome event is also the most frequent act of worship. It is at once the "source, center and culmination of the life and liturgy of the Church"[1] — her heart — and "our daily bread." The Church lives by the Eucharist. When we get down to bedrock, the Eucharist contains, as St. Thomas wrote, "the whole mystery of our salvation."[2]

If asked the straightforward question "Why do you belong to the Catholic Church?" millions would undoubtedly answer: "Because in the Church I receive the Bread of Life." Converts to the faith invariably feel drawn to this central act of Catholic worship. Christ's real presence in the Eucharist is also "a magnet drawing lost sheep home and keeping would-be strays from the deathly snows outside."[3] They know it is the Mass that matters.

The Church community initiates her new members by bringing them to the Eucharist, the goal of her sacramental life. In the Eucharist, we find a continual echo of baptism and confirmation. Only with First Communion does one become completely Catholic, fully incorporated into Christ, an heir to the promise of eternal life (cf. John 6:51), and bodily resurrection (cf. John

6:54). Belonging to the Church, which offers the Eucharist, gives one a right to trust that the Lord will make good on these promises.

The incarnation, the Son's becoming man for our salvation, shows us how much God wants to give himself. This "emptying out" of the Son, "who, though he was in the form of God, did not regard equality with God as something to be exploited" (Philippians 2:6) continues to be made present at Mass. "The humanity of Jesus — his 'flesh and blood' or his 'life' (John 10:15) — is thus, even from the incarnation, eucharistically determined," writes Hans Urs von Balthasar, "inasmuch as it is the bodily gift of God to the world."[4] Neither Christ's resurrection nor ascension reverses the incarnation. He does not abandon us on our pilgrimage, since "he who was once given, slain on the cross, poured out, pierced, will never again take back his gift, his gift of himself."[5] In the Eucharist, the risen Lord continues to give himself for us and for our salvation. It is the pledge of God's irreversible gesture to remain with us until the end of the world.

Receiving the Eucharist is fittingly connected with forgiveness of sins. How often in the Gospels Jesus celebrated divine pardon by banqueting with those forgiven! The merciful father beckoned his servants to kill the fatted calf saying, "Let us eat and celebrate; for this son of mine was dead and is alive again; he was lost and is found!" (Luke 15:23-24). Festivity follows reconciliation. That's why the Church teaches the necessity of confessing grave sins before receiving Communion — lest we do so unworthily. St. Paul wrote, "Examine yourselves, and only then eat of the bread and drink of the cup" (1 Corinthians 11:28).

Sacrifice of Christ

More vividly than any other doctrine, even the incarnation, the Eucharist affirms the "bodiliness" of the Catholic faith. It secures the reality of the incarnation in a radical, yet simple, way. At the Eucharist the very body of Christ becomes present in our midst. While "spiritual" religions direct us to seek salvation by escaping from the world, the Church steers us back to earth.

Refusing to regard the body as a desacralized tool of the spirit, without value, the Church celebrates on her altars the bodily presence of Christ. She understands that flesh and spirit are friends. "Through the flesh," writes von Balthasar, "the spirit gets to know and savor the most precious and priceless things in life, be they joyful or sorrowful, experienced in solitude or in community with others."[6]

We relate to others and to the world through our bodies. We give our bodies to others, as in marital love, or for others, as in saving them from harm. Thanks to the body we can truly express ourselves. Through his becoming flesh the Son of God expressed himself, poured himself out, for us. He spoke, and continues to speak, in bodily terms; that is, he hands himself over to us bodily: "This is my body, *which is given for you*" (Luke 22:19; my emphasis).

The Eucharist reveals the spousal love of God for his people. As bridegroom, Christ "has given himself." His body has been "given," his blood has been "poured out" (cf. Luke 22:19-20). In this way, he loved us to the end (cf. John 13:1). The "sincere gift" of Jesus' self contained in the sacrifice of the cross becomes present in this sacrament of our redemption. "The Eucharist makes present and realizes anew in a sacramental manner the redemptive act of Christ, who 'creates' the Church, his body," wrote John Paul II.[7]

One peculiarity of Catholic teaching on the Mass is revealed in how we refer to it — the holy *sacrifice* of the Mass. This notion of sacrifice is essential to Catholic understanding of the Eucharist.[8] Its celebration is studded with references such as "this holy and perfect sacrifice," "the acceptable sacrifice which brings salvation to the whole world" — and many others. It is firmly established in the Church's prayer and faith that the Eucharist is a sacrifice.

Christ's saving death and resurrection took place once and for all in history (cf. Hebrews 7:27). His death on the cross, the culmination of his whole life of obedience, was the one, perfect, and sufficient sacrifice for the sins of the world. The Eucharist renews this one oblation that Christ offered to the Father on the altar of the cross, by making it present so that even now we can be recipients of its saving power. Christ continues to pour out his Spirit when the Eucharist, the same sacrifice as Calvary, is celebrated. He gave us the Eucharist, says Vatican II, "in order to perpetuate the sacrifice of the Cross throughout the ages until he should come again, and so to entrust to his beloved Spouse, the Church, a memorial of his death and resurrection."[9] The Mass is Christ's sacrifice placed into the Church's hands. United to him, she can offer to the Father what is of greatest value — the sacrifice of the eternal Son.

Bodily Presence

Our sacramental encounter with Christ in the Eucharist is always intimately personal. He is not present to us side by side, as when we sit next to someone at the movies, nor merely in a true communion of spirit, as when we think fondly of someone we love. His is a bodily presence to us, corresponding to our makeup as body-soul beings. His love is not just word, but becomes flesh, becomes body for us.

Of the many interpretations that have been, and could be, given to Jesus' word — that is, "This *is* my body" — the Church has unwaveringly understood this at face value.[10] A simple litmus test of the Church's belief in this real presence can make this clear. What are the elements before consecration by the priest? They are only bread and wine and nothing else. What are the elements after consecration? By the power of the

Spirit they are the body and blood of Christ and only him. The Eucharist does not merely cause what it stands for, as poured water remits sin in baptism, but *is* what it stands for! The appearances of bread and wine signify food and drink, but after the consecration the Eucharist *is* Jesus who becomes our food and drink. In his fourth-century *Catechetical Lectures*, St. Cyril of Alexandria explicitly taught this doctrine of the real presence in his instruction to converts: "The bread and wine of the Eucharist were simple bread and wine before the invocation of the holy and adorable Trinity, but when the invocation has taken place the bread becomes the body of Christ and the wine the blood of Christ."[11] When professing her belief in Jesus' Eucharistic presence, the Church affirms a reality, and not just an individual's thoughts *about* reality.

More than baffling, the realism of Catholic teaching shocks our sensibilities. It brooks no softening into being interpreted as a merely symbolic presence or simple reminder of God's love. Many disciples who first heard Jesus say that his flesh was "true food" and his blood "true drink" (John 6:55) were scandalized. They found his teaching not merely difficult but offensive, and so they "turned back and no longer went about with him" (John 6:66).

"Unless you eat the flesh of the Son of Man and drink his blood, you have no life in you" (John 6:53). The Church unhesitatingly teaches *that* this is true. *How* it can be so remains a mystery, but it is a mystery about which the Church has taken great care to guarantee that its marvel will not be diluted or compromised.

For a long time she did not concern herself with trying to explain in any detail how Jesus became present. But, when after nearly a thousand years, some theologians bandied about certain opinions that would have contradicted her practice of adoring Christ in the Eucharist, she formulated her response in the language in which the question was raised. To affirm her belief in this unique presence, she distinguished it from Christ's presence in the gathered community, in the proclaimed Word, and in the priest representing Christ. Adapting to her own purpose a terminology that had its roots in Aristotle, she taught that, after the consecration at Mass, the "substance" of bread and wine became the "substance" of Christ's body and blood. What happened, therefore, was a change of substance.[12] Despite the technical nature of this vocabulary, the word substance simply designates *that which is*.

In 1215, Lateran IV decreed that "the bread changes into his body by the divine power of *transubstantiation*, and the wine into blood."[13] In the sixteenth century, to clarify the Church's teaching with respect to the Protestant Reformers, the Council of Trent declared that "after the consecration of bread and wine our Lord Jesus Christ, true God and true man, is *truly, really and substantially* contained in the august sacrament of the Holy Eucharist under the appearance of those sensible things."[14]

Transubstantiation is the particular substantial change which refers to that of bread and wine into Christ's body and blood. As long as she uses the language of "substance," the Church must affirm her full faith in the real presence as transubstantiation. Only the appearances, or "accidents," of bread and wine remain after the consecration — nothing else. Though shape, color, texture, etc., are not changed, the body of Christ does *not* exist along with the bread, since a true conversion of substance has taken place. Were this not true, then the Church's Eucharistic worship would be idolatrous![15]

In celebrating the Eucharist, the Church invites her faithful to this intimate closeness of Christ that pierces our being to its very core. Reflecting upon Catholic belief in the Eucharist, Peter Kreeft has written: "It has ceased to scandalize me, though it has not ceased to amaze me, that Almighty God suffers me to touch him, to move him and eat him! Imagine! When I move my hand to my mouth with the Host, I move God through space. When I put him here, he is here. When I put him there, he is there."[16] Such tenderness is an act of love that has proved itself by Jesus' deeds of flesh and blood.

Holy Communion

Memories of a Catholic childhood inevitably include those of one's First Communion. The catechism answers proudly learned by heart, the endless drills in the church, the white dresses, bows, and cakes — all of these things impressed on us the importance of this day. And it did. Every Catholic I know, including those who entered the Church as adults, remembers his or her First Communion. Did we fully understand what was happening? Of course not. But then who ever can grasp the astonishing realism and wonder of the Eucharist?

Belonging to the Church graces us with the Bread of Life. I need that Bread to enjoy eternal life, even now. Without the Eucharist I would simply shrivel up, a withered branch cut from the life-giving sap of the Vine. Celebrating the Eucharist and receiving Holy Communion is "the culmination of the spiritual life and the goal of all the sacraments."[17] When we participate in the Mass by receiving Holy Communion, we obtain the "fruits of the filial reconciliation with God" that Christ has himself gained for us and continually makes present in the Eucharist.[18]

Through the body and blood of Jesus the recipient encounters the living Christ who gives himself to the communicant. This divine *self*-giving is an undeserved gift. In the Eucharist, Jesus does not just share his thoughts, wisdom, and love with us. He shares his very self — in a way even more intimate than spousal love.

Although by baptism a Christian is "in Christ," the Eucharistic presence intensifies this. St. Cyril of Alexandria calls the communicant a "Christbearer." This union with the sacramental body of Christ lasts only as long as the accidents of bread and wine, but a permanent sense of mutual belonging to each other remains: "Those who eat my flesh and drink my blood abide in me, and I in them" (John 6:56). When Jesus said at the last supper that he was "the true vine" (John 15:1), he was not referring just to the passing act of the Eucharistic meal, he was also "claiming a presence in every moment of his disciples' lives, a presence by which he communicated to them his own life, which would become theirs and which would ensure fruitfulness."[19] What food brings about in our bodily life, Holy Communion does in our spiritual life.[20] Through the food of the Eucharist Christ's eternal life imbues human life. We come to share in the divinity of Christ who came to share in our humanity.

Jesus says to us, "In me, God's Word-Made-Flesh, you are destined to be freed from the narrow confines to lead a new life, together with others and share with them, a life of *communion*, a life as befits members of my body, nourished by the circulating blood of my all-embracing self."[21] By sharing the Eucharist, the believer becomes rooted in love. Christ's love overflows in those who welcome him.

Not only does the Eucharist increase our love for God, it is also "a remedy to free us from our daily faults and to preserve us from mortal sin."[22] This gift is for sinners. The more we are absorbed into the Eucharistic mystery, the less hold the glamour of sin has on us. Jesus assures us of his triumph over the world, his victory over despair, chaos, and sin. Confidence, as well as optimism and hope, should flow from sharing the Eucharist. Receiving Communion is a source of joy.

Building Up the Church

The Eucharist fosters not only personal communion with Jesus but also with the Church. Nourished by the Lord's body and blood, the Church becomes ever more what she already is:

the body of Christ. "Because there is one bread, we who are many are one body, for we all partake of the one bread" (1 Corinthians 10:17). St. Augustine saw this relationship so clearly that he could write: "So if you yourselves are the body of Christ and his members, then on the Eucharistic table lies your own mystery. . . . You shall be what you see, and you shall receive what you are."[23] When we eat the Eucharistic bread, which unites us personally to Christ, we also are joined more closely to one another in the Church.[24] By receiving the body of Christ we become the body of Christ, the Church. Although always an intimate experience, like all experiences of authentic love, sharing the Eucharist is not an individualistic or privatized affair.

"Our union with Christ, which is a gift and grace for each individual," wrote John Paul II, "brings it about that in him we are also associated in the unity of his body which is the Church."[25] From our union with the head flows our union with the body. Eucharistic Communion strengthens our bonds with one another and deepens the unity of the Church.

Eucharist with Others

By belonging to the Catholic Church we submit ourselves to a discipline of worship. In a society soaked in "feel goodism," even religion can become a self-help institution where worship focuses on self-fulfillment. Genuine Catholic Eucharistic piety, however, compels us to surrender our self-interest and to unite ourselves with Christ in his sacrifice. That's why the Mass is so crucial. It's not just the time to feel good about the community that warmly welcomes us but to enter into a mystery. It far surpasses anything as banal as just enjoying one another's company. At the Eucharist we give glory to God, not to ourselves or the assembled community. We are not Catholics because we like group coziness and conviviality.

Unlike certain churches with free-flowing liturgy, worship in the Catholic Church is structured and orderly, expressing God's transcendence and our dependence upon him. Since praise is the person's primary duty to God, our Eucharist must give God glory. Any weakened sense of God as Other reduces or minimizes this God-centered character of the liturgy. If we become too focused on ourselves, or on building up community for its own sake, then we have compromised something essential in our tradition.

Since the Second Vatican Council the "conscious participation" of all the faithful in the Mass has been a constant theme of liturgical reform. We pray not just as individuals *in* the Church, but *with* the Church, as members of the body of Christ. Because of its public, official nature, the Eucharistic liturgy demands our involvement. But don't reduce active participation to singing, reading, responding, shaking hands, and then chatting over coffee and doughnuts. True participation is first of the heart. Nor is the Mass a "clerical preserve" — or for those who assume clerical pretensions. The vitality of a Christian community is not measured by how many people are in the sanctuary!

Having recaptured the Eucharist as a communal prayer, even Catholics are sometimes tempted to turn it into an experience of community itself, into "warm fuzzies" that maximize feeling good about themselves. Some even judge how "good" a liturgy is by measuring the participants' "reactions." Such celebrations of the Eucharist are dependent on the "creativity" of its manipulators who often go to great lengths to mount spectacular productions contrived to impress the participants. Yet the Mass is not of our own making. It is Christ's offering that is taking place and to which we join ourselves. Cardinal Joseph Ratzinger has commented that "to most people the liturgy seems to be rather something for the individual congregation to arrange. . . . Imperceptibly, the distinctions between liturgy and conviviality, liturgy and society, become blurred."[26] What the liturgy celebrates is the holy God's coming to us *through* the community, which is its servant and not its sovereign.

External attitudes of respect and devotion help us to participate fruitfully in the Mass. Flowing from the Catholic emphasis on the incarnation and the role of the body in salvation history, kneeling, bowing, and other gestures are natural to us. They are perfectly in keeping with a bodily religion that mediates God's love to us through an incarnational-sacramental plan of salvation.

Because the Church reflects what she believes in how she worships, bishops and the Pope are rightly solicitous about safeguarding the integrity of the Mass. This concern derives from its being the public and official prayer of the entire Church. The Eucharist is not a private function but a Church celebration of God's people united with their bishop and the Pope. That's why we mention their names at every Eucharist. This means that the way we celebrate Mass is not something the individual congregation decides. In its tradition of public worship, Catholicism escapes the manipulation of individuals, whether clerical or lay. When celebrated with noble simplicity, dignified sobriety, and tranquil solemnity, the Eucharistic liturgy can provide a refuge from vulgarity and clamor.

Eucharist for Others

The vigor of the Church's action in society flows from the Eucharist. At Vatican II, the Fathers noted with dismay the phenomenon of Sunday Catholicism: "One of the gravest errors of our time is the dichotomy between the faith which many profess and the practice of their daily lives."[27] Although Christ's kingdom is not "from this world" (John 18:36), the Church rejects the secularist agenda to marginalize Christianity. This view, which colors much of American culture, allows religion to set up shop and stay in business as long as it keeps itself separate from the "real world." Confined to its own little unreal corner, religious people are free to do as they please. To succumb to this divorce between Church and world would be disastrous for Catholicism. In confronting the overwhelming complexity of contemporary problems, we must resist the comfort of a religious ghetto by refusing to separate the Eucharist from our activity in the world. That's why the Mass ends with a dismissal to go forth into the world.

By sharing in the Eucharist we receive the motivation and strength to live as true Christians, to follow in the steps of Jesus' sacrificial love for humanity.[28] Eucharistic Communion enables us to put into practice the new commandment of love we received at the last supper: "Just as I have loved you, you also should love one another" (John 13:34).

Through Christ's intimate Eucharistic bond with us, we receive the strength to commit ourselves ever more generously to following Christ's example, who in this sacrament lays down his life for his friends (cf. John 15:13). United to him and to others, "he sends us into the whole world to bear witness, through faith and works, to God's love, preparing the coming of his kingdom."[29] To be nourished by Jesus as the Bread of Life means that we must ourselves become body and bread for the world. Unless it is to be empty ritual, communion with Christ commits us to renouncing self-love, replacing it with service to the community. As servants, we are not greater than our Master.

Because the Eucharist makes present Christ's obedient death, it also makes available the power of this love for the communicants. Having been so loved, we ourselves can love more intensely. In receiving Communion, we are taken into this "school of active love" for neighbor. It teaches us how to love. As unstintingly as Christ gives himself to the Father for us, so must we give ourselves for the brethren. "If our Eucharistic worship is authentic, it must make us grow in awareness of the dignity of each person," writes the Holy Father. "The awareness of that dignity becomes the deepest motive of our relationship with our neighbor."[30] By sharing in the Eucharistic bread we commit ourselves to sharing our daily bread as well.[31] Not to do so renders our worship sterile and in vain.

Pledge of Bodily Resurrection

The "bodily" thread that runs through Catholicism, from creation, incarnation, visible Church, and sacraments culminates in the Eucharist. Herein Christ, the risen Lord, is made present through transformed bread and wine. These "things" are changed into the glorious reality of Christ's body and blood, the firstfruits, the source and center of a transfigured universe.[32] The Mass is a true foreshadowing, even an anticipation, of the universal glorification to be fully revealed when he comes again in glory to hand over the kingdom to the Father (cf. 1 Corinthians 15:24).

Jesus' saving action is not limited to saving human souls but extends to the whole of creation. In the new creation, matter will be freed from its present limitations and glorified (cf. Romans 8:19-22). Holy Communion, like the Mass itself, directs us to final fulfillment, as a foretaste of the coming kingdom of God. The early Fathers spoke of Holy Communion as the "seed" of bodily immortality that would come to full flower in the resurrection of the body — our final destiny. As a "pledge of our future glory and of our everlasting happiness,"[33] receiving the Eucharist directs our gaze to the eternal kingdom.

In the heart of the Church beats the reality of Jesus' Eucharistic presence. When asked why he belonged to the Church, Hans Urs von Balthasar answered straightforwardly: "Why do I remain in the Church? Because it alone, as the Church of the apostles that knows what is meant by a commission from the Lord and by service to the Lord, can offer me the bread and wine of life. . . . I want to receive the blood of life as the offering of God who in his Son sets before me his total love, which is poured out really in history, irrespective of any attendant circumstances and regardless of the attitude which I as the recipient may assume."[34]

Belonging to the Catholic Church gives one free access to the Eucharist. "The Church's biggest drawing card is not what she teaches, crucial as that is, but who is there. 'Here is here! Therefore I must be here'."[35]

Bodily Truth: Sex and the Catholic Church

THE CHURCH'S INSISTENCE ON THE GOODNESS OF REDEEMED CREATION, of which the Eucharist is the supreme example, has spinoffs in her teaching about the body and sex. As long as we preach the reality of the incarnation and the mediation of the visible Church, what we do with our bodies is a religious question. By belonging to the Church we do not just commit ourselves to belief and worship but to a way of living that touches our sexuality and our pocketbook.

Christianity is focused on the Word made flesh. This divine embodiment is the heart of Catholicism. It should be more of a comfort than a surprise therefore that the politically correct questions of the day, both in the Church and in the world, revolve around sex and justice.

Though it is impossible to provide a complete treatment of human sexuality in so short a book, to neglect mentioning it would be dishonest. Why I belong to the Church *does* have something to do with her teaching on sex. Given society's ridicule of Catholic teaching on sexual matters, it is countercultural to propose that her wisdom in these areas is a convincing reason for staying on board Peter's bark.

That the truth about the human person is accessible to all clear-thinking people cannot be doubted. Today, however, a kind of conspiracy is at work in society that is manipulating us and promoting a mass sexual obsession without precedent. Fortunately God's wisdom and word have enlightened our path. I believe that the clarity of the Church's vision follows from her teaching on the incarnation — God's invasion of our world.

In her sexual teaching, the Church affirms that our "embodiedness" is something to be thankful for. Christ's body, scourged and glorified, was after all the instrument of our salvation. The body of Christ (which is the Church and his Eucharistic body) and our sexual bodies are all linked together in God's plan. To despise one is to despise the others. To revere one is to revere the others.

Fascination with sex is as old as the human race. Thomas Howard says that "it is exceedingly difficult to find a tribe anywhere, or an era ever, that has had no consciousness of sexuality as being a hot potato, as it were."[1] Catholics are no exception. Our faith takes with joyful seriousness the mystery of the incarnation — and so of sex.[2] God uses the human body as a sacrament, a visible sign, to make his love present in our world. The body is our gate to salvation. Whenever we are tempted to exclude the material from our belief and practice, the Church resoundingly replies "no." Precisely as sacred, sex is a matter for religion, since it enters the story of God's relation with humanity.

The Bible itself lays the groundwork in telling us how to live our sexuality according to our dignity as human persons. Once we understand the role of the body in God's plan for our salvation, the vision behind the Church's sexual teachings emerges. Our human and sexual dignity are rooted in God's creating us in his image and likeness (cf. Genesis 1:27).[3]

In this "very good" creation, God gave us more than one language to speak. Besides the gift of speech, he gave us our body. This body expresses itself through gestures that are themselves a language. Just as our verbal speech reveals who we are, so also does our body language. The Lord intends that we speak this "sexual language" truthfully. Regrettably we can lie with our bodies as well as with our tongues. What God thinks about premarital sex, divorce, and contraception, he began to tell us at the dawn of creation. He asked us to speak the sexual language of our bodies truthfully.

Image of God in the Body

The first question about the body arises at the Bible's beginning. "What does it mean to be made 'in the image of God'?"[4] Most of us would respond by saying something about "being spiritual" or "having a soul." To be sure, we mirror God because we are self-aware persons, endowed with an intellect to know and a free will to love. This common teaching is correct. But it does not go far enough. Even in our sex-sated and health-conscious culture, most of us still think that the body is, if not evil, at least irrelevant to God's saving plan.

Yet such worldly-wise thinking does not surpass Plato's view of the body as the prison of the soul, to be shuffled off so that we can arrive at the heavenly court. The "benevolent dualism" of pagan antiquity, where the soul met the body as inferior, is alive and flourishing.[5] "Promotion" to noncorporeal angelic status at the end of life is still the secret wish of many. As in science fiction, which presents more intelligent life as an ephemeral or ghostlike reality, we assume that the higher the spiritual life, the less important the body is. Higher intelligences are rarely bodily and, even more rarely, sexy. These science-fiction beings are the modern-day equivalents of disembodied spirits. Noble as angels are, we shall never join their ranks. We are constantly enticed into minimizing our bodies, thereby trivializing our sexuality.

Such a view is not adequate insofar as it omits any mention of the body or sex. In daily life, the body seems all-important. It brings pain and pleasure, of which sexual pleasure is the highest form. So we have a problem. What is most desirable in life seems to have nothing to do with how we image God.

Unlike dualism's total disdain for the body, many contemporaries merely play down the saving dimension of our sexual actions. Only the spirit counts: *why* we do something, not *what* we do. Sexual acts derive their meaning from our intentions, they say, not from what we do with our bodies. Stressing the intentions behind sex is healthy when it reminds us that we need to live our sexuality with purity of heart. It takes a bad turn, however, if it implies that the moral goodness of sex can be divorced from bodily actions.

God wills to save us, to bring us to himself, through the created material world he has given us. Because God created us in his image *with a body*, we express and receive love through that body. It gives us the means by which to show our love for others and by which they reciprocate our love.

Sex "in the Beginning"

The Christian understanding of human sexuality starts with the Old Testament accounts of creation and the Fall (cf. Genesis 1—3). Although modern biophysiology can tell us something about sex, we must still draw our knowledge of the personal dignity of the human body and sexuality from what God has told us. Adam and Eve, before the Fall, give us the model for living our sexuality.

According to the second account of creation (cf. Genesis 2:4—3:24), Adam was initially alone. Amid the wonder of creation he experienced an agonizing loneliness that God sought to alleviate: "It is not good that the man should be alone; I will make him a helper as his partner" (Genesis 2:18). Alone he was incomplete. Experiencing this original solitude, Adam recognized that his humanity was radically different from the rest of creation (cf. Genesis 2:20). No other being offered Adam the possibility of a relationship of mutual giving.

Adam's *body* marked him as unique, making him conscious of being alone. He recognized that he could express his love for another only in and through his body. Yet the first man lacked someone else to love in that bodily way. In his original loneliness, Adam — the "person" — was not yet aware of his maleness, since his body lacked complementarity. The image of God was not yet fully present in creation, since the human body as both male and female together constitutes this image. The triune God is not "sacramentalized" by a nonsexual being but by male and female. Like the divine persons in whose image he was created, Adam — with his body — was destined to live with others. He yearned to receive the bodily gift of another person and to give himself bodily to another.

Eve was created for Adam, just as Adam was created for Eve. Genesis records Adam's exuberant delight at this discovery. When he awakes from his deep sleep, he does not refer to Eve's powers of thinking and willing but instead cries out, "This at last is bone of my bones and flesh of my flesh" (Genesis 2:23). Commenting on this passage, Pope John Paul II says that Adam seems to say: "Here is a *body* that expresses the 'person'!"[6]

To be a person during our earthly pilgrimage is not only to be a body but to be a body that is sexual. God's remedy for Adam's original loneliness was sexual differentiation. Man and woman are attracted to each other because of their spiritual and bodily dimensions.

Although each was an individual with inherent dignity, the Lord calls man and woman to live together as a communion of persons. We discover our own humanity only with the help of another human being. Alone we do not completely realize ourselves. This happens only by existing *with* someone, and even more deeply and completely, by existing *for* someone.[7] Man therefore recognizes and finds his own humanity with the help of woman just as woman discovers the fullness of her humanity with the help of man.

The unity of Adam and Eve replaced the solitude of Adam. In the Pope's happy turn of phrase, the body has a "nuptial meaning." Because of its sexual differentiation, it can express the unique love by which a person can make a gift of himself or herself to the other. This gift is to be total, selfless, free, and without constraint or compulsion. As nuptial, the body has "the capacity of expressing love: that love precisely in which the man-person becomes a gift and — by means of this gift — fulfills the very meaning of his being and existence."[8] The human vocation to love is fulfilled when one exists in solidarity with others, as a gift for the other, thus imaging the triune Creator.[9]

This mutual bodily gift of Adam and Eve tells us that only by unselfish giving of ourselves to another can we discover ourselves. Precisely because of their complementary masculinity and femininity, man and woman can enjoy communion with each other through their bodies. When each gives him- or herself to the other, both are mutually enriched: receiving the bodily gift of the other and giving the bodily gift of oneself. When two married people as a true communion of persons make love, their one flesh wondrously manifests their creation in God's image.

Before the Fall, Adam and Eve did not experience disorderly sexual desire. True delight in each other's bodily presence was dominated by the will. Sexual harmony existed in this state when the first humans "were naked" and yet "were not ashamed" (Genesis 2:25). Their nakedness expressed chastity, proper sexual ordering, not abstinence. Without seeking sexual pleasure for its own sake, they enjoyed it gratefully as a consequence of their love. The original couple did not separate the lover's body from the other's total person.

Body Language

The body, precisely as male and female, is integral to God's sacramental plan of salvation. It is a kind of sacrament, the expression of the whole person, making visible what is invisible: the spiritual and the divine. God gave us bodies "to transfer into the visible reality of the world the mystery hidden since time immemorial in God, and thus be a sign of it."[10]

Sexual relations are a kind of "body language" through which man and woman carry on that dialogue which had its beginning on the day of our creation. Intercourse enables husbands and wives "to express to each other all that they wish to say in the way of love and spiritual union."[11] To understand our sexuality it is worthwhile to think about our sexual gestures as bodily words that indicate whether we are honest people or liars.

Whenever we speak sexually, our expressions — like all conversations — are subject to the demands of truth, that is, to the will of God. Our sexual "words" — the actions we use to embody our love — can say something either true or false. Honesty demands that our sexual gestures should mean what they say. Our body language ought to express that God-given meaning truthfully. In sexual matters, such honesty is called chastity, an expression and fruit of life according to the Spirit.

On the darker side, because of original sin, our sexual body language can now be dishonest.[12] When so spoken, it falsifies what creation reveals to us about our masculinity and femininity. Deceitful sexual activity frustrates communion between persons. In the Scriptures, the shame attached to nakedness symbolizes sexuality gone askew (cf. Genesis 3:7). Adam and Eve clothed their nakedness because they no longer trusted each other, hiding their visible femininity and masculinity. Because of the Fall, we are now prey to "telling lies" with our bodies. Our hearts have become "a battlefield between love and lust."[13]

When lust entered human relations, the ability to express love truthfully became precarious. If dominated by lust, man and woman seek each other only for gratification. Lust depersonalizes the person by making him or her an "object" for the other. We are all heirs to this "fallenness." Because of paradise lost, our sexuality lacks its spontaneous original harmony.

Sex "in the New Creation"

Yet, despite the Fall, we can still speak a truthful body language "inscribed in the depths of the human heart, as a distant echo of original innocence."[14] For those who are baptized into Christ as a "new creation" (2 Corinthians 5:17), purity of heart can overcome the legacy of lust. Fallen humanity can still discern truth from falsity in its body language and can speak it in either way.[15]

We can therefore live our sexuality as God intended it in the beginning. Why? Because of Christ's redemptive incarnation. He has imprinted on the body of every man and woman a new dignity, since in him the human body has been united, together with the soul, to the eternal Son of God.[16] Insofar as we are now "in Christ," in his body, our sexuality shares in that restoration. His redemption also bears fruit in our bodies, freeing us from the bonds of lust.[17] With the power of God's grace, we can be faithful in living our sexuality as planned in the beginning and restored by Christ.

As we are painfully aware, telling the truth is still difficult for us. It is just as tempting to lie with our bodies as with our tongues. The Church's wisdom provides a splendid vision of sexual integrity. I believe that belonging to the Church commits us to living our sexuality in ways frequently at odds with conventional social norms. Neither prospective converts nor cradle Catholics should be shielded from confronting these questions. The Church's teaching on premarital sex, divorce, and contraception is not a set of edicts that could be changed at will; rather, it articulates the truth about the body and its sexual language. This truth is based on human nature — on who we are and what sex is. We didn't design our nature, so we can't make up the guidelines. They are "the unchangeable rules of the operating manual," says Peter Kreeft, "written by the Designer of our human nature."[18]

God gives us his greatest gifts *through* his creation — beginning with Christ and continuing in the Church and through her sacraments. The material, here the bodily, is ennobled and raised to being an instrument of divine life. Grace is given with material mediation. If the sacramental economy is to "work," we must use signs and symbols. In sexuality, therefore, intercourse has a symbolic meaning to be respected. It both reveals ourselves to others and reveals who God is. *How* we speak our sexual language is crucial.

Premarital Sex as a Lie

Sexual relations can speak fully and truthfully only within the permanent and exclusive commitment between husband and wife. God brought us forth as man and woman, as husband and wife. That is what Adam and Eve were to each other: friends, spouses, lovers, parents-to-be. Honest sexual language requires a pledge of permanent fidelity. The "one flesh" (Genesis 2:25; Matthew 19:5; Ephesians 5:31) the lovers become symbolizes a permanent commitment, impossible outside marriage. Consequently, premarital sex is fundamentally dishonest.[19]

To entrust your body to someone else is "a real symbol of the giving of the whole person."[20] No act between man and woman is more intimate. The gift of the body symbolizes the sincere and total gift of self. Yet this gift cannot be given when the couple is unmarried. In this case, the partners are saying one thing with their bodies — "I love you totally and definitively" — but another with their wills — "I love you now but will commit to nothing permanent." The two "words" are contradictory.

Premarital intercourse is a lie because by their bodily union the partners are saying that they belong totally and irrevocably to the other. By its very nature love should be unconditional. Yet, because they choose not to be married, their bodily gift of self is transient and incomplete. They reserve the possibility of deciding otherwise in the future. Whether explicitly voiced or not, each retains the right of having sexual relations with someone else in the future. Neither partner is really fully giving his or her total self to the other during premarital sex. Without a pledge of permanence, sexual relations are a lie. Truthful body language demands a total commitment to the other, a commitment that includes the precious gift of one's future.

The more casual the premarital sex, the more such relations express the "replaceability" of the other. According to John Paul II, such intercourse really involves "carrying out an 'experiment' with human beings whose dignity demands that they should be always and solely the term of a self-giving love without limitations of time or of any other circumstance."[21] In premarital relations, the body of the other becomes a means of self-gratification, a body-for-me in the present. Premarital sex is a lie because it robs one's partner of his or her dignity and of the right to be totally accepted in the gesture of bodily entrusting.

Adultery and Divorce

In a similar (though more serious) way, adultery entails deceitful body language. What the partners are saying with their bodies — "I am wholly yours, you are mine forever" — they know is untrue. At least one of them has already given him- or herself to a spouse in this way. The gift of the body, meant to be a total gift of self to the other, cannot be realized in adulterous relations. Adultery lacks "the character of the truthful sign."[22]

The sexual language of the body helps us to understand why the marital bond should last until the death of one's spouse. When Jesus taught that no one can divide what God has joined (cf. Matthew 19:6), he insisted that sexual language be restored to its authentic beginning. The two who become "one body" verbalize the unity and indissolubility of marriage as expressed in creation and renewed by Christ.

Christ will never divorce his Church; nor will the Church ever abandon her Lord. Likewise spouses cannot break their covenant relationship as long as they are both alive. As "one flesh" they should not be divided.[23] The Lord's fidelity to his one bride, despite her faults and infidelities, also explains why marriage should be monogamous, between one man and one woman, and indissoluble. Drawn into this mystery that binds Christ to his Church by their marriage (cf. Ephesians 5:22-33), husband and wife are bound by a similar covenant. As a sacramental entity, conjugal relations symbolize and truly make present Christ's eternal love for his Church. Their marriage must therefore be as permanent as that enduring love of Christ. The language they speak in their acts of conjugal love necessarily demands fidelity and permanence. If they lack this intention, their body language is false.

Contraception as Contradictory Love

When God "rested" after the work of his creation, he entrusted to the newlyweds the dignity of prolonging his work, of becoming co-creators with him (cf. Genesis 1:28). As fruitful as God's love is, so must a husband's and wife's love be for each other. Their unity in "one flesh" is essentially linked to the blessing of fertility.[24]

God's eternal trinitarian love is life-giving and reaching beyond itself. Because both husband and wife exist for the other in interpersonal communion, their mutual bodily gift "opens to the gift of new life, a new human being, who is also a person in the likeness of his parents."[25] Their child comes into being from their bodily love. Sexual union oriented to children symbolizes and brings into existence the communal structure of society, built up through family relationships into more complex communal structures. That's why the family is society's "basic cell." While giving themselves bodily to each other, the spouses "give not just themselves but the reality of children, who are a living reflection of their love, a permanent sign of conjugal unity and a living and inseparable synthesis of their being a father and a mother."[26] Conjugal love has an inherent dynamism toward motherhood and fatherhood.

We cannot speak two contradictory languages with the body — one of love and another of unfruitfulness — and remain honest. Catholics *believe* that the life-giving and love-giving meanings of our sexual language are inseparable. In his prophetic encyclical *Humanae Vitae* (1968), Paul VI unequivocally affirmed that every marriage act must remain open to the transmission of life. This teaching, he attested, "is founded on the inseparable connection, willed by God and unable to be broken by man on his own initiative, between the two meanings of the conjugal act: the unitive meaning and the procreative meaning."[27] John Paul II has reaffirmed his predecessor's teaching. Even more, he proposes that the Church's teaching on contraception "belongs not only to the natural moral law, but also to the moral order *revealed by God*."[28] How we express our bodily language so that it respects this fruitfulness is a pressing moral question.

All arguments favoring contraception accept that a couple has the right to separate the procreative from the unitive meaning of conjugal relations. The Church replies that this willful divorce of what God has joined in sexual relations is immoral. Although those endorsing contraception maintain that it does not compromise the conjugal act as love-giving, this is not so. God has given to man and woman a sexual language to express total love. Intentionally to suppress potential parenthood introduces a contradiction into conjugal love. In contraceptive intercourse, says the Pope, couples "act as 'arbiters' of the divine plan and they 'manipulate' and degrade human sexuality — and with it themselves and their marriage partner — by altering its value of 'total' self-giving."[29] In short, contraception distorts the language of the body.

By resorting to contraception, married couples deny that their sexual language should express a love that is total. Pope John Paul II has written: "Thus the innate language that expresses the total reciprocal self-giving of husband and wife is overlaid, through contraception, by an objectively contradictory language, namely, that of not giving oneself totally to the other. This leads not only to a positive refusal to be open to life but also to a falsification of the inner truth of conjugal love, which is called upon to give itself in personal totality."[30]

Because in contraceptive intercourse the partners withhold the procreative power of conjugal love, they refuse to give the full gift of their masculinity or femininity to the other. The spouses violate the truthful communion that their sexual relations should reveal. Without this truth, their body language is false. When contracepting, one neither gives nor receives the full bodily gift of the other, a gift that includes possible parenting.

In truthful intercourse, couples either will to share their generative power or, as in natural family planning, they accept their periodic unfruitfulness. The nuptial gift of the body, which involves surrender of one's entire self, including one's fertility, is not total if they contracept. What appears to be a "complete" marital act is, in fact, stunted through deceit. Contraception obstructs the truth, because while you are giving your bodily and spiritual self to the other, you are also saying, "I do not love you totally, because I reject your fertility." Almost alone among Christians, the Church valiantly condemns contraception because it cannot express the divinely given truths that our sexual body language is meant to reveal. Like a voice crying in the wilderness, she calls her faithful to speak bodily truth.

Telling Nothing but the Truth

By belonging to the Catholic Church, we have access to the full truth about the human person. Her teachings on sex are not arbitrary, impersonal, and changeable; instead, they are anchored in the word of God first manifested in creation and restored by Christ's teaching and grace-giving sacrifice. The Church's moral norms on sexual questions emanate from God's wisdom, from what is truly good for us. If we do not recognize the divinely given bodily truth about ourselves, then our sexual expressions cannot be fully loving. To communicate using authentic body language, the believer must be willing to subject him- or herself to the demands of truth, to that profound reverence due to the person created in God's image and likeness.

As we prepare to begin the third millennium, the Catholic Church will confront forces more and more hostile to her vision of sexuality. As we look forward with hope, we are also afforded the opportunity to look back to "the beginning." Neither prudish nor puritanical, the Church teaches the whole truth about the human person. Her wisdom concerning sexual behavior is not based on an outdated anthropology and psychology but on a liberating revelation of sexuality that will set us free for one another and for the kingdom. Belonging to the Church engages us in courageously living this bodily truth.

Belonging to the World

A CURIOUS PARADOX OF CATHOLICISM IS THAT ITS PASSIONATE CONcern for eternal life does not obscure taking this world seriously. I am proud of the Church's outreach in her vast array of health-care, educational, and other social-service agencies. At the same time, I am wary of a simpleminded humanism that would identify working for social justice as the principal purpose of the Church.

As only she can, the Church walks a tightrope. Keeping her gaze fixed on the heavenly Jerusalem, the kingdom that is "not from this world" (John 18:36), she is immersed in this world God loved so much that he gave his only Son to save it (cf. John 3:16). To belong to the Catholic Church sets us in the midst of an exciting challenge: pursuing justice with all our might, yet knowing that its fulfillment will come only in the future reign of God.

Catholicism encourages a commitment to meeting people's material needs because it emphasizes the corporate and the bodily. It also refuses to play off hope for the heavenly world against concern for this world. The Church tends all members of the body of Christ — whether Catholic or not — because to do so is to care for Christ.

Priorities

No doubt about it. We have a supernatural vocation that transcends the limits of this world and reaches to heaven. The Church's primary purpose is to lead us there. This mission she jealously guards and fosters. The love of Christ impels her (cf. 2 Corinthians 5:14) to proclaim the good news of this destiny when "we will be like him, for we will see him as he is" (1 John 3:2). The *Baltimore Catechism* was right on the mark. God made us to know, love, and serve him in this world and be with him in the next.

While rejecting every attempt to reduce her mission to a worldly goal in which people strive only for the temporal good of others,[1] the Church also recognizes that she has a charge to humanize the world. She is to promote the good of the whole person, first as a member of the city of God, and then as a member of the earthly city.[2] The order here is crucial. "Because God's love has been poured into our hearts through the Holy Spirit that has been given to us" (Romans 5:5), believers must *therefore* bear fruit in acts of love. Since divine grace transforms us, we in turn must transform the world. We are told that "faith without works is . . . dead" (James 2:26).

What does this mean for the Church? She is God's instrument of grace and mercy to the world. The Church has the task of encouraging the faithful to renew the world by promoting human dignity. Like Christ, the Church announces salvation to the whole person, to one's whole bodily and transcendent existence, not only in the world to come but also beginning here on earth.[3] Followers of Christ therefore have a responsibility to this world. Action on behalf of justice is "a constitutive dimension of the preaching of the Gospel."[4]

Social Doctrine

God's initial covenant with humanity occurred when he created man and woman as the first community, the family. In his image, they were created for communion with others — as we saw in the preceding chapter. But God's command was twofold. Men and women were also to subdue the earth (cf. Genesis 1:28) for the good of its inhabitants. God destined the earth and its resources for all peoples.

Tragically sin entered the world and disrupted its original harmony by introducing greed, exploitation, and selfishness. With the grace of Christ's saving death and resurrection, however, we can reclaim creation as it was intended at the very beginning. Guided by justice and inflamed by charity, our goal is to assure that everyone shares equitably in all created things.[5] Since creation is the Lord's, its fruits belong to all creatures, without exclusion or favoritism. To assure a fair sharing of these divine gifts is the work of justice.

In his ministry, Jesus himself did not focus on social questions such as "the universal destination of the earth's goods."[6] That came later. He was not a social reformer in the traditional sense. Nonetheless, he planted seeds for his followers to harvest. It was up to them to discover ways to feed the hungry, clothe the naked, and care for the sick (cf. Matthew 25:31-46).

Nor did it take Christians long to garner the firstfruits of Jesus' teaching. Living their baptism, they quickly came to see that the gift of the Spirit had ramifications for their lives in the world. St. Luke records how seriously the early Christians at Jerusalem took their social obligations: "There was not a needy person among them, for as many as owned lands or houses sold them and brought the proceeds of what was sold. They laid it at the apostles' feet, and it was distributed to each as any had need" (Acts 4:34-35). Incorporation into the body of Christ entailed living in the world in a radically new way.

As time passed, and people's experiences accumulated, the Church sought to put Jesus' teaching into practice amid different political, economic, and social situations. The Church's social teaching was born from the encounter between the Gospel message and social problems. What slowly emerged was a set of principles and practical guidelines that we call *social doctrine*.[7] The Church now has at her disposal a body of teaching that, like all tradition, has matured gradually through time. Guided by the Holy Spirit, she has interpreted the world's shifting situations in light of the Gospel. Throughout this development the Church has held steadfast to her right to influence public life with her religious and moral teachings.

Spearheaded by the popes, this teaching has developed rapidly since the first great social encyclical of Pope Leo XIII, *Rerum Novarum*, published in 1891. Being Catholic today means accepting the social doctrine taught in papal encyclicals, the documents of Vatican II, bishops' statements, and the *Catechism of the Catholic Church*.

All such documents clearly distinguish between *principles* enunciated and *policies* proposed to implement them. In its essential principles, this social doctrine is normative for believers. Respect for human dignity (especially the inviolable right to life), justice, peace, etc., are not negotiable. Yet, because social teaching is oriented toward action, the ways in which its goals are implemented will develop in response to history's changing conditions. New policies will replace older ones that are no longer able to embody Gospel principles.

As an "expert in humanity," the Church's magisterium has the duty of analyzing social realities, making judgments about them, and then recommending just responses to problems.[8]

To do this the Pope and bishops draw on the wisdom of human sciences. What principally guides them, however, is the light of faith and the Church's tradition. Their primary task is to propose principles that can guide social, political, and economic realities. Their secondary duty is to evaluate whether the specific structures of a particular time and place conform to Gospel teaching. By her social doctrine the Church seeks to help the faithful apply God's word to their daily lives.

Sometimes the magisterium makes specific recommendations about *how* human dignity could best be preserved in a given situation. Such judgments, however, are not meant to be definitive, and individual Catholics are free to foster the same principle in the way they judge best. It is a principle of Catholic social teaching, for example, that everyone has a right to a sufficient amount of the world's goods to live a decent life. How this is to be best achieved is primarily the laity's task, even if the

Pope and bishops recommend certain actions. In other words, when studying social doctrine, Catholics must carefully differentiate between the *principles* taught as revealed truths and the *concrete applications* suggested for putting them into practice.

Human Dignity

Belonging to the Catholic Church involves more than professing orthodox beliefs. It includes holding distinctive beliefs about the human person. In their social doctrine, Catholics have a rich treasure — a true anthropology founded on the person of Christ. Because of creation and redemption, we have the resources to explore reality and to find solutions to the deep-seated problems that beset us.[9]

The heart of all Catholic social teaching is its view of human dignity. From Leo XIII's *Rerum Novarum* to John Paul II's three social encyclicals — *Laborem Exercens* (1981), *Sollicitudo Rei Socialis* (1987), and *Centesimus Annus* (1991) — the Church has sung a single tune. One basic theme — an unshakable affirmation and vigorous defense of the dignity and rights of the human person — has been, and remains, the linchpin of Catholic social teaching.

The Church does not possess a collection of recipes on the specifics of running a government or managing the global economy. Her principal contribution to the political, economic, and cultural order is her vision of human dignity. Walking with humanity through history, she gives it direction by safeguarding the transcendence of persons.[10] To ignore this vocation to immortality strips people of their dignity and ultimately leads to the slavery of abusive power, unbridled lust, and socially destructive greed. Without this openness to transcendence, a true vision of who we are is stifled.

By creating and redeeming us, God has guaranteed our dignity. From creation itself humanity enjoys an inestimable value.

Perched at the summit of creation, the human person is the only earthly creature whom God has willed for himself and destined for grace and glory.[11]

Because of this nobility, each human life is unique, sacred, and endowed with an inherent dignity that God alone freely confers. No human creation exists that is not the image of God. Nor can human dignity be negotiated. Having its unshakable foundation in God as Creator and Father, human dignity cannot be lost by crime or sinfulness. Yet how often we compromise this dignity in hospitals, at work, and in the trenches!

Having its roots in creation, human dignity comes to full bloom only with the light of Christ. The Son of God has re-created us and enlightened us about the heights to which God has raised us, the surpassing worth of our own humanity, and the meaning of our existence. With the incarnation, God affirmed our dignity in the loftiest way possible. We are brothers and sisters of God's own Son! In one of Vatican II's most memorable passages, the Council Fathers wrote that "by his incarnation, he, the Son of God, in a certain way united himself with each person."[12] He intensified this union by his saving death and resurrection for us. Christ shed his precious blood for everyone, thereby uniting himself with each person through his redemption.[13] Human dignity rests therefore on the solid foundation of creation by God and of salvation by Christ. Because of this dignity, *every* individual must be treated as a person — and never an as object to be used or as a means to an end.[14] Furthermore, any discrimination that divides and degrades the human family is an intolerable injustice that inflicts dishonor on a person's dignity.[15]

Rights Embody Dignity

Once we recognize the *fact* of human dignity, certain consequences for daily life follow.[16] We champion this dignity by respecting, defending, and promoting human rights. Everyone is meant to enjoy these God-given and inviolable rights. No individual, group, authority, or state, can alter — let alone justly eliminate — them. Why? Because such rights find their source in God himself.[17] He alone is their author. If rights are not based on this inherent dignity of persons with a transcendent vocation, any list of them — from the Bill of Rights to the Universal Declaration of Human Rights — would be an arbitrary collection that could change at whim.

Most social doctrine aims at specifying the implications of human dignity in every major area of social life: religion, politics, family, culture, and economics. Without claiming to be exhaustive, the American bishops have compiled a list of such rights: "Flowing from our God-given dignity, each person has basic rights and responsibilities. These include the rights to freedom of conscience and religious liberty, to raise a family, to immigrate, to live free from unfair discrimination, and to have a share of earthly goods sufficient for oneself and one's family. People have a fundamental right to life and to those things that make life truly human: food, clothing, housing, health care, education, security, social services and employment."[18]

Although believers might disagree about the best way to embody these rights in concrete situations, the rule that orients Catholic action is simple: Every social, political, economic, or social policy is to be evaluated by how well it promotes the dignity of the human person.

Solidarity

Today many people are confused about what it means to be a person and are floundering in their search for meaning. They propose an exaggerated individualism that focuses on the person isolated from the community. Fulfillment is to be found, they say, in isolation from others, unrelated to any community outside the self. The individual is a self-contained reality that exists and acts by itself without reference to any community, culture, or society. "Hell is other people," declared the French philosopher Jean-Paul Sartre.

Searching for one's individual identity and self-fulfillment have become, for many, life's principal objective. Slogans buttressing this mentality, such as "Look out for number one" or "You deserve it," are all too familiar. This way of thinking has also infiltrated the pews. Communal institutions, including the family, are decried as constraining the autonomous and sovereign individual. The bitter fruits of this individualism as compensations for tragic loneliness are hedonism, frenetic consumerism, and flight from social responsibilities.[19]

According to Catholic social doctrine, personal fulfillment is achieved by pursuing the *common* good.[20] Pope John Paul II calls such responsibility toward others *solidarity.* This new buzz word, associated with the workers' movement in Poland that initiated the downfall of communism, comes from the Latin *solidare* — "to make solid, to join firmly together." According to the Pope, solidarity is not "a feeling of vague compassion or shallow distress at the misfortunes of so many people, both near and far"[21] but a sense of moral responsibility to and participation in the life of the community.

God did not create the human person to be alone but for interpersonal communion. In order to flourish as persons — to have life in abundance (cf. John 10:10) — we must reach out to others. What the biblical tradition teaches about being created for communion with others, human wisdom confirms. The ancient Greeks and Romans described the human person as a "social animal" made for friendship, community, and public life, with a duty to promote the common good.

Despite our living in a global village, serious obstacles to true solidarity are woefully evident. This "communion of sin" shows itself in the intolerable poverty of hundreds of millions, the widening gap between the so-called developed North and the developing South, and the selfish isolationism of prosperous communities indifferent to those in need. All breeches of solidarity compromise humanity's God-given unity. They cry to heaven for justice.

Solidarity opposes both individualism (which denies our nature) and collectivism (which reduces us to objects of state, social, or economic interests). As a firm and persevering determination, solidarity commits us to our neighbor's good.

Belonging to the Church therefore is not like taking out membership in an organization with narrowly defined obligations. Including a sense of compassion and responsibility for others but not restricted to this, solidarity makes our charity concrete, the distinguishing mark of Christ's disciples (cf. John 13:35). It involves the specifically Christian traits of total gratuity, forgiveness, and reconciliation.[22] The spiritual and corporal works of mercy express a solidarity that Catholic individuals and communities are both called to practice. Solidarity makes us willing to confront the structures of power and greed that threaten society with the Gospel's liberating truth. It invites us to live and work *for* others and *with* others. This chain of solidarity begins within the family and radiates to the community, nation, and world.

Preferential Option for the Poor

The Catholic Church has a long and distinguished record of solidarity with the poor. Millions of believers have imitated Christ by living poor, simple lives. In addition, countless others have cared for the involuntary poor through Church-sponsored good works. In doing this, Catholics followed the example of the early Jerusalem Christians who distributed their possessions so that "there was not a needy person among them" (Acts 4:34).

Reaffirming this ancient tradition, the present Pope urges Catholics to embrace a preferential option for the poor: "In fidelity to the spirit of the Beatitudes, the Church is called to be on the side of those who are poor and oppressed in any way. I therefore exhort the disciples of Christ and all Christian communities — from families to dioceses, from parishes to religious institutes — to carry out a sincere review of their lives regarding their solidarity with the poor."[23] Genuine solidarity demands that we attend to the poor.

Nor are middle-class Catholics with shrinking disposable income excused from this evangelical call to serve those most in need. Besides directly helping the poor, they are to "go public" for them.

In their 1986 pastoral letter, *Economic Justice for All*, the American bishops explained this kind of solidarity: "Decisions must be judged in light of what they do for the poor, what they do to the poor, and what they enable the poor to do for themselves."[24] The standard to use in judging economic, political, and social policies is simple: They must be at the service of all people, especially the poor. Solidarity with the poor is not icing on the Catholic social cake. It is essential to Church membership.

Subsidiarity

Enshrined within Catholic social doctrine on human dignity is also the principle of subsidiarity. When applied to social life, it promotes solidarity by encouraging an individual's participation in and responsibility for the common good. Although Pius XI first formulated this principle in his encyclical *Quadragesimo Anno* (1931), John Paul II provides us with an up-to-date definition: "A community of a higher order should not interfere in the internal life of a community of a lower order, depriving the latter of its functions, but rather should support it in case of need and help to coordinate its activity with the activities of the rest of society, always with a view to the common good."[25]

Subsidiarity attempts to regulate how institutions, from the family to the state, relate to each other. The principle favors decentralization. Higher authorities — whether political, economic, cultural, or educational — ought not to absorb or take over what lower levels of authority can do equally well or better. If you can get it done in the neighborhood or local level, then do it! This is the Catholic application of the well-known saying "Small is beautiful."

Individual responsibility, personal freedom, and creativity are encouraged when subsidiarity is taken seriously. This bias toward smaller groups fosters the development of real communities of persons who interact, plan responsibly, and carry out common projects. By preventing society from becoming an anonymous and impersonal mass, these small communities strengthen and "personalize" the social fabric. Attention to subsidiarity prevents totalitarian and collectivist institutions, even in a democracy, from dominating communal life.

Family

Among all social institutions, the family enjoys pride of place. Promoting family values is a major concern for Catholics. God himself gave the family its mission of being society's fundamental unit.[26] When healthy, it assures both human dignity and solidarity; when diseased, innumerable personal tragedies inevitably result and social collapse is never far away. I am convinced that "the future of humanity passes by way of the family."[27] The Church's social doctrine will never bear fruit in the wider community unless its lessons are first learned in this primary social cell.

The family should exist neither in isolation from other communities nor merely serve as a safe refuge from a turbulent world. As Church we must denounce a family egoism that concentrates exclusively on its own internal life. The family must not withdraw into itself but should be an instrument for humanizing and personalizing other communities. Social obligations are therefore integral to its vocation. Among these is the family's duty to further a social order that maximizes personal freedom by forming individuals open to serving wider communities and animated by a sense of social justice.[28]

As society becomes increasingly depersonalized, we find that things, efficiency, and technique become more important than people. This process can be reversed only by refocusing on human dignity. In the family, one first becomes aware of his or her dignity by learning what it means to love and to be loved — what it means to be a person.[29] Here children meet the first "others": parents, siblings, relatives. Integrating members into society begins in the family.

The family is the primary place where children are guaranteed security and are protected from the dog-eat-dog world of inhuman competition. By recognizing the human dignity of each member, despite age or usefulness, the family helps to make possible a society based on true human dignity. As "the first and irreplaceable school of social life," the family provides a model and stimulus for communal relationships that are "marked by respect, justice, dialogue and love."[30] It humanizes society as a leaven working from within.

When family life is based on shared communion, genuine solidarity exists. Often our neediest brothers and sisters are within our own family. To respect and care for them teaches us how to treat others, thereby overcoming crippling hyper-individualism with its "me first" whining. If we fail to develop family solidarity, however, communities and nations will inevitably pursue their own narrow self-interest, indifferent to their neighbors' needs.

As society's essential cell, the family is the subject of rights and responsibilities before any other community. Here subsidiarity means that the state should not take away from the family any functions that it can carry out just as well on its own or in other free associations, like parent and neighborhood groups.[31] Instead, the state should positively favor and encourage family initiatives. When the Church urges families to take subsidiarity seriously, she discourages any government, even if benevolent, from assuming total control over the family's own responsibilities.

To the detriment of subsidiarity, other major institutions have increasingly assumed many functions that American families used to perform. Health care, education, recreation, and even catechesis have slipped away from family control. Yet the principle of subsidiarity requires that it should be recognized as society's first agent of education, its primary health-care provider, and its principal teacher of religious values. According to Catholic social doctrine, the family, with help from other institutions for what it cannot do on its own, best meets these needs. Parents should understand, for example, that they cannot delegate their educational duties to any other institution: to school, state, or parish. These institutions should complement families and assist — not supplant — them if they are unable to fulfill their charge.

Revitalizing society and the Church begins with the family. If family life and values are debased, then society becomes corrupt, the Church's work of evangelization suffers, and human dignity will be compromised. If the family is strong, it will foster human dignity, solidarity, and subsidiarity.

Laity in the World

The front-line troops in the Church's mission to promote human dignity are lay men and women. Their pursuit of holiness is realized by their life in the world. Nothing should replace the laity's primary mission in marriage, family, work, science, economics, culture, and politics. Unfortunately in America we are presently experiencing a new form of flight from the world — the temptation to concentrate all our efforts on the Church's internal life.

Since Vatican II, lay Catholics have been mesmerized by seeking out "ministries" *within* the Church. But the lay vocation is not best served by bringing it into the sacristy. What specifically characterizes the laity is its secular nature. The Council Fathers at Vatican II insisted that laypeople have their own proper vocation: to seek the kingdom by engaging in temporal affairs and to order them according to God's plan.[32] Their life in the Spirit expresses itself by involvement in the world's affairs.[33] They are to permeate the world with the Spirit of Christ and to imbue all dimensions of culture with genuine moral values.[34] Catholics, along with other men and women of good will, should work for the betterment of this world. To animate the temporal order, Catholics ought not to relinquish participating in public life but should play their part in the economic, social, legislative, administrative, and cultural sectors that promote the common good.[35]

Teaching her social doctrine belongs "to the Church's evangelizing mission and is an essential part of the Christian message."[36] Armed with this teaching, Catholics have sure guidelines for bearing witness to Christ in the world.

Our Man in Rome

POPE JOHN PAUL II FILLS THE WORLD'S STAGE. HE FASCINATES PEOPLE with his magnetic appeal, whether forgiving his foiled assassin, receiving Gorbachev in the Vatican, comforting the sick, or crowning a statue of Mary. Easily the world's best-known personage, the Pope is admired and loved, ridiculed and loathed. His office compels attention. Neither the pomp of the British monarchy nor the power of the American presidency captivates Americans as much as the Roman papacy.

It testifies to the Pope's importance that people supporting every conceivable cause try to elicit his support. Every Catholic wants the Holy Father on his side. Though the Pope might be derided, he is not ignored. John Paul II strives to use this backhanded compliment to his influence in his favor. Unlike a politician or a professor, he does not criticize his opponents directly. Though he preaches the Catholic faith without apology or compromise, the Holy Father prefers to win over his adversaries by persuasion, geniality, and patience. He has been very successful not only in strengthening the faith of Catholics but in inspiring many to deepen their love of God.

A Catholic's identity is intimately tied to the bishop of Rome. "When asked what makes them different, what is distinctive to themselves, Catholics point, first of all, to the papacy," wrote Avery Dulles. "Because of its importance as a symbol of Catholic identity, the papacy is, for Catholics and for others, laden with such emotion."[1]

In many places, including the United States, Catholics were often called "papists." Loyalty to the Pope distinguished them from other Christians in the playground and in politics. Catholics were proud of having their "man in Rome" as vicar of Christ. Although in recent years this intense pride has faded, being Catholic still means believing that Christ gave the papacy to the Church as an essential ministry. So crucial is the Pope that without his leadership the Church would not be what Christ intended.[2] Belonging to the Church brings with it the glory, burden, and blessings of the papacy.

Jesus and Peter

Why is the Pope so vital to Catholic identity? To answer that question we must go back to Jesus' call of Peter. The Pope exercises a ministry that has its origins at the Church's beginning, when the Lord gathered his band of disciples around himself. Although John Paul II was not on the shores of the Lake of Galilee or at Caesarea Philippi, the office he holds is rooted in the extraordinary friendship between Jesus and Peter.

When Jesus told Simon that he would "fish for people" (Matthew 4:19), a unique Master-disciple relationship began. Jesus counted on Peter. He entrusted this impetuous fisherman with a mission that he wanted to continue in the Church "to the end of the age" (Matthew 28:20). Despite his weakness, Peter accepted this burden. Like Mary, Peter also made his *fiat* (cf. Luke 1:38), renouncing himself and entrusting himself entirely to the Lord.

On three distinct occasions, Jesus picked out Peter *alone* and confided to him a unique role among his disciples. The evangelists record these dialogues in the so-called *Petrine texts* found in the Gospels of Matthew, Luke, and John. Though singled out from the other apostles, Jesus' special words to Peter occurred *with* them present.

The most renowned exchange took place in Caesarea Philippi. In response to Simon's confession of his Master's identity, "You are the Messiah, the Son of the living God" (Matthew 16:16), Jesus solemnly made him the foundation of his new community: "And I tell you, you are Peter [that is, Rock], and on this rock I will build my church" (Matthew 16:18).

For the Jews, giving a new name marked a decisive moment

in salvation history. In the Old Testament, God changed Abram's name to Abraham (cf. Genesis 17:5) and Jacob's to Israel (cf. Genesis 32:28). In each case, the name change indicated a divine choice and function for the one selected.

This also happened to Peter. After Peter professed who Jesus was, Jesus says who Peter is.[3] Until this episode, no Jew had been called Peter. God transformed shaky Simon into steadfast Rock. Because of God's choice, Simon became Peter and was to assume specific duties in the new community, a role that corresponded to his new name of "Rock."

Undeniably Christ Jesus himself is the Church's "cornerstone" (Ephesians 2:20), but he wanted Peter to bear the name and exercise the authority that was his from the Father. Peter was vicar of the rock. In the mid-fifth century, Pope St. Leo the Great aptly paraphrased Jesus' words to Peter, leaving no doubt that the apostle depended upon the Master: "I am the foundation and no one can lay any other. And yet, you, Simon, you also are a Rock because I am going to give you my strength, in such a way that, by this sharing, the power that is only mine will be common to you and to me."[4] Jesus made Simon Peter a sharer in his own mission to found the Church on solid rock.

Nothing could be clearer than Peter's utter dependence on Jesus in his vocation to be the Church's visible foundation. Without God's help, the apostle is only "flesh and blood" (Matthew 16:17). In this tension between the Lord's gift of solidity and Peter's own capacities, we have "an anticipation of the whole drama of the papacy's history."[5] Even when individual popes become a rock of scandal, because they try to precede Christ and not follow him, Peter's successors remain the Church's visible foundation. Like Peter, they have often been brutally addressed: "Get behind me, Satan! You are a stumbling block to me; for you are setting your mind not on divine things but on human things" (Matthew 16:23).

So that Peter could fulfill his foundational role, Jesus promised to equip him with the authority he would need: "I will give you the keys of the kingdom of heaven, and whatever you bind on earth will be bound in heaven, and whatever you loose on earth will be loosed in heaven" (Matthew 16:19). As the master of the house controls entry to it, so does Jesus, the Door (cf. John 10:9), open the gate to the kingdom. In handing over its keys to his chief steward, he designates Peter to be its "doorman." Only Peter — and he alone — receives supreme authority to open and close the doors that give access to heaven. That's why to this day the "keys" of Peter are found on monuments, souvenirs, and, more seriously, why we refer to papal authority as the "power of the keys." It also explains the endless "pearly gates" jokes with Peter dutifully opening or barring the doors of heaven!

Peter's power to "bind and loose" specifies the authority transferred with the power of the keys. This language comes from that used by Jewish rabbis at the time. It means that Jesus granted Peter full authority over the Church's doctrinal and disciplinary affairs. The apostle could do whatever would be necessary to make Church life flourish.

St. Luke records the second commission that Jesus assigned only to Peter. During the last supper, just after he had foretold the apostle's denial, Jesus assured him by a special promise: "I have prayed for you [Peter] that your own faith may not fail" (Luke 22:32). Elsewhere Jesus prays for the other disciples and for all his followers (cf. John 17:9-20). Yet, on the night before he died, he guarantees to Peter that his faith will not fail. Even the apostle's foreseen sin of betrayal could not cancel the efficacy of Jesus' prayer. The steadfastness of Peter's faith, like all his "privileges," depends totally upon divine grace and not on his own strength.

Because Christ assured that the gates of hell would not undermine Peter's faith, the apostle received another charge: "And you, when once you have turned back [repented], strengthen your brothers" (Luke 22:32). Like all gifts of grace, this one too entailed a mission for others. Since Jesus' prayer personally supported him, Peter was told to share that strength with others by affirming their faith. On every pastoral visit he makes, Pope John Paul II cites these words to explain the religious meaning of his pilgrimages. Sustained in his frailty, the Pope is impelled to teach the faith in every circumstance, to instill courage in the faithful, to comfort those in doubt, and to lead nonbelievers to the truth.[6]

St. John's Gospel narrates the last intimate encounter between Jesus and Peter — this time after Jesus' resurrection. To complement Peter's earlier confession of him as the Messiah and to forgive his weakness in denying him, Jesus now elicits from him a threefold profession of love. The apostle's positive response to the repeated question "Do you love me?" is followed by the charge "Feed my lambs" and "Tend my sheep." The last time Jesus says, "Feed my sheep" (John 21:15-17). By this triple repetition, a form that the rabbis used to signify a solemn transferral of authority, Jesus revealed his will regarding the community's future structure.

The Good Shepherd himself (cf. John 10:11) passed his pastoral staff to his chosen disciple. He authorized Peter to be his vicar in tending the people of God. As Jesus shared with Simon his quality as "rock," so here he communicates his mission as "shepherd." But the sheep remain Christ's. The Church is the Lord's, not Peter's! After Jesus' departure, those responsible for the early communities were also called shepherds (cf. Acts 20:28; Ephesians 4:11), but the Lord singled out Peter to watch over his whole flock.

What is entailed in Peter's pastoral ministry? Commenting on this text, John Paul II writes: "As a shepherd leads his sheep to where they can find food and safety, so the shepherd of souls must offer them the food of God's word and of his holy will (cf. John 4:34), ensuring the unity of the flock and defending it from every hostile attack."[7] Here again the power of divine grace shines through. Established to forgive sins — "I have come . . . to call sinners" (Mark 2:17) — the Church is a wounded community whose members need reconciliation. In his person, Peter represents both that need and the divine response of healing. Although holding the keys of the kingdom, the shepherd must take the lead in asking for and receiving forgiveness.

Peter and the Apostolic Community

What Jesus asked of Peter, the apostle carried out. He was the rock, affirmer, and shepherd of the early Christian community. With the Lord's promises ringing in their ears, the first believers recognized that to ignore Peter's guidance would compromise the heritage Jesus had left them. Scriptural witness to his leadership abounds.

Among the disciples who announced the good news of the resurrection, Peter became its *official* proclaimer. In the most ancient creedal formula we have recorded, St. Paul gives Peter this pride of place when he points out that Christ "was raised on the third day in accordance with the Scriptures, and . . . he appeared to Cephas [Peter] and then to the Twelve" (1 Corinthians 15:4-5). Paul does not dispute that the women were the first to believe in the resurrection and tell others, but he highlights the fact that it was Peter's proclamation that strengthened the first followers' faith. St. Luke makes the same point. When the two disciples returned from Emmaus to tell the Eleven that they had seen the risen Lord, they were greeted with the exultant refrain: "The Lord has risen indeed, and he has appeared to Simon!" (Luke 24:34).

Scripture amply testifies to Peter's preeminence in the apostolic Church. After Judas' death, Peter noted the vacancy among the "Twelve," called an election for his replacement, and laid down the criteria to be used in selecting him (cf. Acts 1:15-26). Later, on Pentecost, Peter preached the Church's *first* great homily (cf. Acts 2:14-36) and continued to "fish for people" by preaching to the crowds (cf. Acts 3:12-26, 4:8-12, 5:29-32, 10:34-43, 15:7-11). Though not the only miracle worker in the apostolic Church, he was also the *first* to use that charism (cf. Acts 3:1-10).

Probably Peter's most historic "primatial" act was baptizing the Gentile centurion Cornelius and his whole household without first requiring circumcision (cf. Acts 10:1—11:18). On his own authority, Peter opened the Church's doors to non-Jews and guaranteed that the Gospel would be preached "to the ends of the earth" (Acts 1:8).

He also played a decisive role at the "council" in Jerusalem when Paul, Barnabas, and "the apostles and the elders" (Acts 15:2) gathered to discuss whether circumcision should be imposed on pagan converts to the faith. Again Peter's word was decisive. Upon hearing him, "the whole assembly kept silence" (Acts 15:12).

Luke also narrates that Peter was the object of special divine intervention and of the community's prayer, as his miraculous rescues from jail testify (cf. Acts 5:19-21, 12:1-11). When imprisoned, "the church prayed fervently to God for him" (Acts 12:5). This prayer arose from a shared conviction of Peter's unique importance. So began the history of the Church's uninterrupted prayer of asking the Lord to protect Peter's successor.

Even the testy Paul, so jealous of his rights as an apostle and presuming to reprimand Peter "to his face" (Galatians 2:11), never questioned the *fact* of his leadership. The Apostle to the Gentiles recognized Peter's authority as a guarantor of his own mission to evangelize the pagans. Three years after his conversion, Paul had gone up to Jerusalem to confer with Peter (cf. Galatians 1:18). Fourteen years later he returned there to confirm that he "was not running, or had not run, in vain" (Galatians 2:2). Paul rebuked Peter for disregarding the decision he had already agreed to.[8] He was not undermining Peter's pastoral supremacy! Precisely because he accepted Peter's authority, Paul felt free to protest his leader's "backsliding" when he compelled Christians of pagan origin to submit to the Jewish law (cf. Galatians 2:11-14).

A venerable tradition exists in the Church for correcting the Pope. In the fourteenth century, St. Catherine of Siena followed Paul's example, castigating the Pope, whom she called her "sweet Christ on earth," for his cowardice in not returning to Rome from Avignon. Even today not every critical word masks an underlying hatred of the papacy. If any Catholic were "Pope for a day," he or she would undoubtedly want to change something about the way the Holy Father does his job. There's no lack of suggestions on how best to give the papacy a face-lift! Such gentle criticisms must, however, be clearly distinguished from that "Pope-bashing" which has become fashionable in certain Catholic circles.

Peter's primacy in the apostolic community is further confirmed by the Scriptures. When the evangelists wrote down the names of the Twelve, they always placed Peter first in their lists (cf. Matthew 10:1-4; Mark 3:15-19; Luke 6:13; Acts 1:13). In summarizing this New Testament recognition of Peter's role, John Paul II writes: "It is clear from these writings that from the Church's beginning Peter exercised decisive authority at the highest level. This exercise, accepted and recognized by the community, is historical confirmation of the words spoken by Christ regarding the mission and power of Peter."[9]

What Happened After Peter?

No explicit scriptural evidence exists proving that Peter went to Rome. This is not surprising. The Bible does not address details of Church structure after the apostolic age. Nonetheless, from the end of the first century, we have documentary testimony of Peter's sojourn in Rome.[10] To that we can add impressive archaeological evidence for the fact that Peter was buried at the Vatican not far from where he was martyred. Today, at this venerable site of martyrdom, Michelangelo's magnificent dome rises over the remains of the apostle's tomb.

As long as Jesus' Church would need a foundation and his sheep tending, someone would have to fill the shoes of the Galilean fisherman. Jesus willed that Peter's mission was to continue. After the apostle's crucifixion under Nero, bishops at Rome took on the responsibilities that Jesus had assigned to Peter. Catholics believe this historical development corresponds to God's lasting will for his Church.

Before A.D. 100, bishops of Rome were acting in ways that showed, even before they fully articulated the reasons, that they had obligations extending beyond the local church at Rome and embracing the universal Church. Over time, this Roman primacy evolved like an oak from an acorn. Nor were these Petrine duties simply claimed by the bishop of Rome. The other bishops, who themselves never dared to take on similar tasks, recognized that communion with Peter's successor, the bishop of Rome, was necessary if they were to be faithful to Jesus' plan for his Church.

Although other churches sometimes disagreed about the precise nature and rights of this Roman primacy, belonging to the Church meant accepting the Pope's ministry. Before the end of the second century, St. Irenaeus summed up Rome's importance: "For this church [of Rome] has a position of leadership and authority; and therefore every church, that is, the faithful everywhere, must needs agree with the church at Rome."[11] When the early Church had to define her faith in face of attacks, Irenaeus answered that the faith of the Roman Church was *the* criterion of the genuine apostolicity and orthodoxy.

In these early centuries, one very significant way the bishops of Rome fulfilled Peter's mission of protecting the unity of Christ's flock was their resolution of disputes that other churches brought to their attention. In the fourth century, St. Jerome wrote to Pope St. Damasus: "I follow no one as leader except Christ alone, and therefore I want to remain in union with the Church and with you, that is, with the chair of Peter. I know that on this rock the Church is founded."[12]

Catholics believe the papacy to be an essential and permanent ministry in Christ's Church. Yet we cannot assume that the papacy as an institution is totally unchangeable. Not every role that the Pope has taken on in history belongs, strictly speaking, to Christ's permanent will. For centuries the bishop of Rome was also a temporal sovereign over the Papal States in central Italy. Helpful as that role might have been at the time in assuring the Church's freedom to preach the Gospel, it is not required by the Petrine ministry willed by Christ. Other examples could be given. While fidelity to God's plan demands that the Pope should fulfill those duties first entrusted to Peter, the Lord did not specify every detail of his job description. Just as in the past the papacy served the Church's changing needs, so will it in the future.

Vicar of Christ

Jesus gave us the papacy as a gift to help us on our journey to the kingdom. Chapter 5 has already explained the Pope's decisive role as the Church's chief teacher. Among the many other functions of the papal ministry are those linked to his sacramental role, ministry of unity, and pastoral authority.

The *Baltimore Catechism* defined a sacrament as "an outward sign, instituted by Christ, to give grace." Since Vatican II, we commonly refer both to Christ and the Church as sacraments. Jesus is the visible presence of God, the Word made flesh, and the Church is the visible body of Christ. For the same reason, the Pope also can be called a sacrament. He is not a replacement for Christ, to be sure; rather, he is a visible representative, a sign of our Lord's presence. For this reason

Catholics commonly refer to the Holy Father as the vicar of Christ.

Rooted in the mystery of the incarnation, the papacy is not just a function to be performed or the chief executive office of a multinational corporation. Christ is the eternal Shepherd who never leaves his flock untended (cf. John 10:11-18). Through the Pope, he continues to watch over, protect, and guide us. In the Pope's actions, Christ himself is audible and visible. As vicar of Christ, the Pope speaks for the Master. "The very voice of Christ himself" reaches listeners, wrote Paul VI, "through the lips and ministry of his representative on earth; indeed, Jesus himself speaks with the accent of his vicar."[13] Of him Catholics can truly affirm that the Pope acts in the person of Christ.[14]

Through his divinely instituted office, the Holy Father gives people the opportunity to encounter Christ. As his vicar, he makes the Lord's love and authority present through his ministry. The popular enthusiasm that characterizes Catholic devotion to the Pope, so evident when John Paul II lifts a baby in the air or comforts a dying AIDS patient, is based on this insight. Holding aloft his crosier with Christ crucified, the Holy Father reminds us that the Pope pastors the Church in the Lord's name and power.

Minister of Unity

As a visible sign of Christ, the Pope is entrusted with preserving Church unity. Merely by his presence he reminds us of Christ's headship of the Church. In our age of rapid change and ferment, disintegration threatens us from every side. A fragmented world cries out for unity. As one charged with ensuring Catholic unity, this papal responsibility is now more necessary than ever.[15]

In the introduction to *Pastor Aeternus*, the document of Vatican I (1870) that defined papal primacy, the Fathers said that Christ instituted this ministry "in order that the episcopate itself might be one and undivided, and in order that the entire multitude of believers might be maintained in unity of faith and of communion."[16] Among the Pope's principal concerns is keeping bishops and people united in the one faith. Simultaneously he is to foster the Church's catholicity and maintain her unity — not uniformity.

The Church herself is to be a sign to the world of the unity of the human family. Unified by the Spirit, she is called to be "an effective leaven of fraternal oneness in the community of the peoples."[17] More than headquarters, Rome is the center of the Church's unity and thereby a light to the world. The Pope fosters this by receiving into communion all other Catholic bishops. By being in union with him, each one is necessarily in union with all others. In this way, the Pope is an active instrument for promoting that unity which is God's will for his people.

Despite this enormously weighty role, the Pope is not a king who rules over the universal Church from above but a father who pastors from her visible center. Bishops who head local churches (dioceses) work *with* the Pope as well as *under* his primatial care. The bishop of Rome is "the living memory for the local churches and their bishops so that all can recognize their identity and their image in him, the leader."[18] The Pope sustains the communion of faith and witness of all churches throughout the world.

Ordinary Catholics show their appreciation for his ministry of unity by flocking to see the Holy Father on his pastoral visits. He does not come as an intruder to the local church but as one who belongs there, who links Catholics throughout the world in confessing Jesus as Lord.

Shepherd and Servant

In our democratic age, authority gets bad press. Some even think that any use of it contradicts the Gospel. Yet, like Christ who taught with authority, so must the Pope. Jesus did not surrender his claim to speak and work with divine authority when he washed his disciples' feet. He claimed no worldly honors. Nor should the Pope. He must imitate the Lord in serving and not being served (cf. Mark 10:45). His ministry is not a pretentious but empty "primacy of honor." That's why Vatican I taught that the primacy held by Peter and his successors is one of "jurisdiction" and not of "honor."[19]

Papal *jurisdiction* is the divinely bestowed right and power given to the Pope so that he can carry out his Petrine duties. The term designates the authority Jesus intended Peter to have for effectively pastoring the Church.

In light of Vatican I's solemn teaching, reaffirmed at Vatican II, we can describe this jurisdiction in the canonical language in which it is still commonly couched. First, the Pope's authority is that of a pastor of souls. It is not the kind of power proper to a king or president but derives from the fact that the Pope is the *bishop* of Rome. His jurisdiction is truly *episcopal*.[20] In the same way that a bishop teaches, sanctifies, and governs in his own diocese, so also does the Pope in the universal Church.

Papal jurisdiction is also *supreme*;[21] that is, no higher authority exists in the Church. The Pope has the last word in all ecclesial matters. He does not have to contend with a Supreme Court that can overrule his decisions!

The Holy Father also enjoys *full* Church authority. Whatever authority Christ left to his apostle, the Pope may exercise. No legitimate ecclesial authority exists that would lie outside his competence to exercise. This does not mean the bishop of Rome should do everything, nor that he should take over the responsibilities Christ has given to bishops. His ministry is to be used only when it is needed — and always for building up the Church.

The Pope receives his pastoral authority directly from Christ. It is not delegated to him from the college of cardinals that elected him, from the episcopal college whose head he is, or from the faithful whom he serves as supreme pastor. Church dogma and canon law call this his *ordinary and immediate* jurisdiction.[22] He has the right to discharge his ministry for the Church anytime, anywhere, and without asking anyone's permission. Though he may wait for an appeal to come to him, the Pope can intervene whenever he thinks it is necessary for the Church's welfare.

Lastly, the Pope's jurisdiction is *universal.* It extends to the Church throughout the world — that is, to all Catholics, whether bishops, priests, religious, or laity. No Catholic can claim that the Pope has "no right to meddle" when the Church's well-being is at stake. According to Vatican I, the Holy Father not only can teach on faith and morals but also can govern the Church and regulate her discipline.[23] His responsibilities therefore extend to all matters of Church life — even those without any claim to permanent truth but that concern good administration. Such affairs include dispensing from religious vows, regulating the law of priestly celibacy, calling an ecumenical council, accepting bishops into communion with him, regulating sacramental celebration, and managing Church goods.

Despite this heavy burden of responsibilities, the Pope may not legitimately exercise his authority capriciously. Like all Catholics, he is bound by Scripture, sacred tradition, and "the ancient and constant faith of the universal Church[24] . . . as it is also contained in the acts of the ecumenical councils and sacred canons."[25] Papal authority is limited by service to Christ and the Church.

The Pope receives Peter's authority for no other reason than to serve the Church. As "servant of the servants of God," he is her supreme pastor. As vicar of Christ, he points to his Master as well as embodies his authority. The Pope carries his burden fully aware that he can be the rock, affirmer, and shepherd only because it is the Lord who sustains his Church.

The ministry of Peter, which continues in the person of the

Pope, is a divine gift that serves to ensure the unity and integrity of the apostolic faith. I am profoundly grateful for this charism that is such a force for goodness, reconciliation, peace, justice, and uncompromising Gospel truth. To recognize the Pope as "our man in Rome" — because he is first Christ's vicar and Peter's successor there — is an extraordinary benefit reaped by belonging to the Catholic Church.

A CONCLUDING CHECKLIST

ALTHOUGH CHECKLISTS RUN THE RISK OF OVERSIMPLIFYING COMPLEX matters, I have yielded to the temptation to draw up one. What follows is a brief summary of my principal reasons for belonging to the Catholic Church. I have settled on ten points, a number that has a long and venerable history in the Christian tradition. Although the list suggests a certain order, beginning with the important reasons, I intend it to be approximate. And, most of all, it is *personal*. This checklist of reasons cannot be given any more weight than one man's reflections!

I belong to the Catholic Church because. . .

✔ ***THE CHURCH GIVES US CHRIST.*** The Church's fundamental mission is to direct us toward the mystery of Christ. She is only the moon that reflects Christ, Light of the nations. As the Savior of all, he is the only one who truly reveals God to us and leads us to him. No one can enter into communion with the triune God except through Christ who is eternally espoused to his bride, the Church.

By accepting Christ as the Church offers him, we open ourselves to the definitive Word who is the cause of our hope, the good news, and the bearer of joy to whom the Church gives testimony. He is the true vine (cf. John 15:5), and we are the branches engrafted on to him so that we may share divine life. By belonging to the Church we abide in Christ without whom we can do nothing.

✔ ***CHRIST GIVES US THE CHURCH.*** Not a screen obscuring access to Christ, the Church is the instrument through which we hear and touch the Word of life (cf. 1 John 1:1). Coming from God and leading us back to him, she is sustained by his constant help. As his body and his bride, Christ has made the Church his vessel, an extension of himself. Just as God chose Mary's womb for the incarnation, so does Christ choose the Church as the place where his life will become fruitful in his followers. Here he has promised to remain forever present to his people.

Because we are incorporated into the Church through baptism, we become the beneficiaries of salvation. Won by Christ at the price of his blood, the Church is his partner in redemption. As the body of Christ in the world, she has been endowed with every grace. The Holy Spirit dwells in her, enlivens her with his gifts, sanctifies, guides, and constantly renews her. Although we cannot exclude God's action outside the Church's visible boundaries, by belonging to her we know God's saving plan for humanity and celebrate it in our teaching, life, and worship.

✔ ***THE CHURCH TEACHES THE FULL TRUTH.*** The Church's faith is not a list of unrelated truths from which we can choose at will. It is a single seamless garment each of whose threads is necessary to maintain its wholeness. Mysteries of faith are woven together so that the garment unravels even if one thread is pulled out. Catholics cannot therefore be selective about official Church teaching. They prize their faith as objective and beyond manipulation, accepting its fullness with gratitude.

Being Catholic means embracing everything that God has communicated to us in Christ. The fullness of this divine revelation extends beyond Scripture alone. The Spirit overflows its pages. Nor did Scripture ever intend to be exhaustive. Revelation's fuller and more profound meaning emerges only in light of Church teaching.

Subjectivism in matters of faith compromises the authenticity of revelation by fashioning a religion of our own making. Belonging to the Church saves us from accepting only what is pleasing, what corresponds to the narrow confines of our own experiences, or what does not challenge how we live. In the depths of our hearts, we yearn for the solid food of God's revelation to set us free. Deliverance from the alienation of discouragement, sin, and death comes when Christ, the Truth, becomes our "way" (cf. John 14:6).

✔ ***THE CHURCH PROVIDES COMMUNAL SUPPORT.*** Believers do not reach out to God in isolation. Never alone, they cling together in the Church and appropriate what she offers. United as members of the body of Christ, they discover that belonging to the Church brings with it the communal wealth of the ages so wonderfully described by Henri de Lubac: "The whole of creation, visible and invisible, all history, all the past, the present and the future, all the treasure of the saints, multiplied by grace — all that is at our disposal as an extension of ourselves, a mighty instrument."[1]

As a communion of saints, the good of all in the Church becomes the good of each, and the good of each becomes the good of all. In the body of Christ, we live in the company of the saints and with them we can come "to know the love of Christ that surpasses [all] knowledge" (Ephesians 3:19). This communion of saints supports us in our weakness, encourages us in times of doubt, and unceasingly intercedes for us.

✔ ***THE CHURCH IS ONE AND CATHOLIC.*** Not one among others, like a denomination, the Catholic Church is both the single source from which all other churches have separated themselves and the point of convergence to which they are all drawn. Despite the trials of history, the Catholic Church has preserved the "one faith" (Ephesians 4:5) of her apostolic origins. Catholics in Rome, Toronto, Lagos, or Bogotá share the same faith.

Yet celebrating this faith in liturgy, theology, and piety shows an astonishing richness and catholicity. Just as society promotes multicultural diversity, so does Catholicism foster the embodiment of its one faith in a marvelous symphony of distinct cultures.

In the history of Christianity, fragmentation and divisions have all too frequently marred the visible unity among Christians. By God's grace, nonetheless, the Church's essential oneness has been preserved in the Catholic Church. The ministry of Peter, now held by the bishop of Rome, has sustained this unity through the ages. This visible principle continues to uphold the Church as a communion of unity in diversity. As the rock and shepherd, the Pope not only assures our Catholic identity, he is in our midst as a servant of the Gospel. We need this divinely given ministry to guide us and keep us from splintering into opposing groups.

✔ ***THE CHURCH HELPS US TO BECOME SAINTS.*** God wills that we become holy, calling each one of us to be holy by imitating Christ. The Father "chose us in Christ before the foundation of the world to be holy and blameless before him in love" (Ephesians 1:4). Although the ways to this perfection of love are many, the Lord has given us his Church as a powerful instrument to help us fulfill our vocation. He died for his spouse that he might make her — that is, us — holy.

Knowing our frailty, Christ gave the Church all the means of salvation necessary for us to live according to the Spirit. Through listening to and meditating on the word of God, through celebrating the sacraments, through the instruction of pastors, and through the witness of personal holiness, the Church showers us with opportunities so that we might come to "see him as he is" (1 John 3:2). The Church helps us become saints because Christ is with her. He is the vine and we are the well-tended branches!

✔ ***THE CHURCH HAS APOSTOLIC AUTHORITY.*** The apostolic authority that Christ left to his followers is still alive in the Catholic Church. Bishops gave us the Scriptures and continue to ordain priests who celebrate the Eucharist for us. Empowered to speak and act for Christ in matters of salvation, these successors to the apostles make present his authority as he promised.

For our benefit the bishops and Pope preserve the Gospel that they have received from the apostles and their successors. Their teaching authority protects us from deviations and simultaneously guarantees the apostolic faith by keeping it free from error.

Through the bishops and the Pope the Church authoritatively preaches the truth of the Gospel without compromise. Not limiting her teaching to social-justice questions often praised by the mass media, she also hammers away at crucial sexual and life issues. By belonging to the Church we are graced with abiding in the truth when faced by fashionable secular opinion. Jesus Christ promised the Holy Spirit to the Church's pastors so that they could fulfill their ministry of teaching the Gospel authoritatively — and, if need be, infallibly — guarding the truth handed down from the apostles and stirring up its power in every age.

✔ ***THE CHURCH REVERES CREATION.*** Reverence for matter and the body runs through God's sacramental plan celebrated in the Church's worship. The body — that of which we are made, to which we owe pleasure and pain, and whose glorious resurrection we await — has been forever ennobled by the Son's uniting human nature to himself in Mary's womb. Through the incarnation God has made the body an instrument of salvation.

Catholicism does not teach that we must denigrate material things. Because it is God's creation, the world is sacred, his dwelling place. Catholics rejoice that God became involved with Adam's clay and the original couple's marital union. Her sacramental worship celebrates the "one flesh" that now exists between Christ and his Church. The God-Man continues to use creation, especially the sacraments, as the door through which we enter into union with the Trinity.

✔ ***THE CHURCH NOURISHES US WITH THE BREAD OF LIFE.*** Before leaving this world, Christ poured out in the Eucharist the riches of his divine love for humanity. Here his life-giving death and resurrection become present for us. Because we belong to the Church, we can receive the "true food" and "true drink" (John 6:55) of his sacred body and blood so that we may have eternal life!

In the Eucharist, the intimate union of Christ and the Church is realized in its fullness. This presence of the body of Christ on the altar is possible because he took the Church as his bride when she came forth from his side at Calvary. Were it not for the Church, we would not have this most precious testament of divine love.

The Eucharist renews the covenant that God has made with humanity through Christ's sacrificial death. It is the sacrament of his love, the sign and cause of the Church's unity, the bond of charity among believers, and the paschal banquet in which we receive the pledge of future glory. This daily bread also propels us to serve our neighbor, educating us in love. Because we belong to the Church we can receive the Eucharist wherein Christ draws us into his self-giving attitude and enables us to surrender our lives in loving service to our brothers and sisters.

✔ ***THE CHURCH FOSTERS HUMAN DIGNITY AND SOLIDARITY.*** Because of her teaching on each person's origin and final destiny, the Church opens us to the whole truth about who we are. God created everyone in his image and endowed each of us with rights that are sacred. By pursuing her supernatural mission, the Church sheds the light of the Gospel on earthly realities. In promoting human dignity, she helps heal human misery and injustice. As an "expert in humanity," the Church offers her social doctrine to serve humanity. Because we belong to the Church, we work in the world hoping for Christ's return, for the coming of his kingdom in its fullness when all will be transformed.

To overcome our selfish individualism, which frequently leads us to flee from accepting social responsibility, the Church calls us to solidarity with others. Enlightened with the word of truth, the Church helps form our social conscience. Communion with the Church leads to solidarity as an authentic service of neighbor.

Our whole lives as Christians come from the Church into which we are baptized, whose creed we profess, and whose mediation strengthens us. The vocation of belonging to the Church is never cause for presumption or pride. To this wondrous call we should respond with amazed and deeply felt gratitude by the obedience of faith: a generous, total offering of ourselves to God, modeled on Jesus' own sacrificial oblation.

I hope that this book has shown that Christ is not separated from his Church. We cannot follow him or live for him, without her. Being Catholic allows us to worship the Lord whose saving graces flow through the Church to all humanity.

Our love for the Church should not be credulous but truly filial. To be called to the Catholic Church is sheer grace, a wonder, a responsibility. Why God chooses us remains his secret. That he has done so calls for our appreciation of this marvelous way he has willed to save us: "To him be glory in the church and in Christ Jesus to all generations, forever and ever" (Ephesians 3:20-21).

CHAPTER NOTES

Note: Numbers with no designations such as 16 in the first note (Introduction) generally indicate pages or chapters and sections — as in the following note (Introduction, Note 2). All others will be identified accordingly, while paragraphs in official documents will be preceded by the # sign. DS (which first appears in Chapter 2, Note 11) is short for Denzinger-Schönmetzer (Henricus Denzinger and Adolphus Schönmetzer), the editors of *Enchiridion Symbolorum Definitionum et Declarationum de Rebus Fidei et Morum*, and will be referred to hereafter simply as DS. Citations from the Vatican II documents (see Chapter 2, Note 15, for example) are taken from various sources, including *Vatican Council II: The Conciliar and Post Conciliar Documents*, gen. ed. Austin Flannery, O.P., Northport, N.Y.: Costello Publishing Co., and Grand Rapids, Mich.: Wm. B. Eerdmans Publishing Co., © 1975, 1986, 1992 by Rev. Austin Flannery, O.P.; *The Documents of Vatican II*, gen. ed. Walter M. Abbott, S.J., New York: The America Press, © 1966; and *Decrees of the Ecumenical Councils*, ed. Norman P. Tanner, S.J., London: Sheed & Ward, and Washington, D.C.: Georgetown University Press, © 1990, as well as the author's own translations. The same applies to other documents (papal and otherwise) — that is, they are gleaned from various sources.

Introduction

1. *Spiritual Journeys*, ed. Robert Baram (Boston: Saint Paul Books & Media, 1988), 16.
2. St. Augustine, *The True Religion*, 7, 2.
3. John Paul II, "Peter Strengthens His Brothers in Faith," *L'Osservatore Romano*, 49 (December 9, 1992), 1.

Chapter 1

1. Congregation for the Doctrine of the Faith, *Instruction on Infant Baptism* (1980), #4.

2. James Hitchcock, "Eternity's Abiding Presence," in John J. Delaney, ed., *Why Catholic?* (Garden City, N.Y.: Doubleday & Co., Inc., 1979), 74.
3. Anne Roche Muggeridge, *The Desolate City* (San Francisco: Harper & Row, 1986), 7.
4. John Deedy, "Why Catholic? Why Not?" in Delaney, ed., *Why Catholic?* 41-42.
5. Rite of Acceptance into the Order of Catechumens and of Welcoming Baptized but Previously Uncatechized Adults Who Are Preparing for Confirmation and/or Eucharist [baptized Catholics] or Reception into Full Communion with the Catholic Church.
6. *The Habit of Being*, ed. Sally Fitzgerald (New York: Farrar, Straus & Giroux, Inc., 1979), 347.
7. *The New Catholics: Contemporary Converts Tell Their Stories*, ed. Dan O'Neill (New York: Crossroad Publishing Co., 1987).
8. Emilie Griffin, *Turning: Reflections on the Experience of Conversion* (New York: Doubleday & Co., Inc., 1980), 59.
9. Cited by David Nichols, "Through the Eyes of Father Neuhaus," *Our Sunday Visitor* (October 25, 1992), 14.

Chapter 2

1. John Paul II, *Message for the 1988 World Day of Peace*, #5.
2. Joseph Ratzinger, "God and Freedom: Jesus, the Way, the Truth and the Life," *Origins*, 19:36 (8 February 1990), 594.
3. Christopher Derrick, *That Strange Divine Sea: Reflections on Being a Catholic* (San Francisco: Ignatius Press, 1983), 126-127.
4. Karl Barth, Epistle to the Romans (New York: Oxford University Press, 1968), 134-135.
5. St. Augustine, *Homilies on the Gospel of St. John*, 27; cf. *Catechism of the Catholic Church*, #158.
6. *Catechism of the Catholic Church*, #150.
7. Karl Rahner and Herbert Vorgrimler, "Faith," in *Dictionary of Theology*, 2nd ed. (New York: Crossroad Publishing Co., 1981), 167.
8. Walter Kasper, *Transcending All Understanding: The Meaning of*

Christian Faith Today, tr. Boniface Ramsey (San Francisco: Ignatius Press, 1989), 16.
9. *Catechism of the Catholic Church*, #145-146.
10. Kasper, *Transcending All Understanding*, 52.
11. "We believe that what he has revealed is true, not because the intrinsic truth of things is recognized by the natural light of reason, but because of the authority of God himself who reveals them, who can neither err nor deceive" (*Dei Filius*, ch. 3; DS 3008); cf. *Catechism of the Catholic Church*, #156.
12. *Catechism of the Catholic Church*, #157.
13. *Catechism of the Catholic Church*, #144.
14. *Catechism of the Catholic Church*, #153.
15. Vatican II, *Dei Verbum*, #5; cf. *Catechism of the Catholic Church*, #153.
16. Allan Bloom, *The Closing of the American Mind* (New York: Simon & Schuster Trade Books, 1987), 25.
17. John Paul II, *Message for the 1988 World Day of Peace*, #1.
18. Peter Kreeft, *Fundamentals of the Faith: Essays in Christian Apologetics* (San Francisco: Ignatius Press, 1988), 174.
19. John Paul II, *Pastores Dabo Vobis* (1992), #7.
20. Derrick, *That Strange Divine Sea*, 143.
21. Hans Urs von Balthasar, *A Short Primer for Unsettled Laymen*, tr. Michael Waldstein (San Francisco: Ignatius Press, 1985), 74.
22. *Spiritual Journeys*, ed. Robert Baram (Boston: Saint Paul Books & Media, 1988), 394.

Chapter 3

1. Hans Urs von Balthasar, *A Short Primer for Unsettled Laymen*, tr. Michael Waldstein (San Francisco: Ignatius Press, 1985), 29.
2. Walter Kasper, *Theology and Church* (New York: Crossroad Publishing Co., 1989), 139.
3. Hans Urs von Balthasar, *In the Fullness of Faith: On the Centrality of the Distinctively Catholic*, tr. Graham Harrison (San Francisco: Ignatius Press, 1988), 22.
4. Vatican II, *Dei Verbum*, #4; cf. *Catechism of the Catholic Church*, #66.

5. Vatican II, *Dei Verbum*, #8; cf. *Catechism of the Catholic Church*, #94.
6. Vatican II, *Dei Verbum*, #4.
7. Vatican II, *Dei Verbum*, #7.
8. Vatican II, *Dei Verbum*, #7-9; cf. *Catechism of the Catholic Church*, #74-82.
9. Yves Congar, *The Meaning of Tradition* (New York: Hawthorn Books, 1964), 172.
10. St. Clement, *First Letter to the Corinthians*, 42; see also Tertullian, *The Prescription against the Heretics*, 21.
11. St. Athanasius, *To Serapion*, 1, 28.
12. Vatican II, *Dei Verbum*, #8.
13. St. Irenaeus, *Against Heresies*, 3, 4.
14. *Catechism of the Catholic Church*, #124.
15. Vatican II, *Dei Verbum*, #18.
16. Vatican II, *Dei Verbum*, #11; cf. *Catechism of the Catholic Church*, #105-107.
17. Vatican II, *Dei Verbum*, #8; cf. *Catechism of the Catholic Church*, #120.
18. Kasper, *Theology and Church*, 139.
19. Michael Schmaus, *Dogma: God and Revelation*, vol. 1 (New York: Sheed & Ward, 1969), 222.
20. Vatican II, *Dei Verbum*, #10.
21. *Catechism of the Catholic Church*, #113.
22. John Paul II, *Centesimus Annus* (1991), #3.
23. Vatican II, *Dei Verbum*, #8.
24. Avery Dulles, *The Craft of Theology: From Symbol to System* (New York: Crossroad Publishing Co., 1992), 99.
25. *Catechism of the Catholic Church*, #83.
26. Dulles, *The Craft of Theology*, 103.
27. Vatican II, *Lumen Gentium*, #8.
28. International Theological Commission, "On the Interpretation of Dogmas," *Origins*, 20:1 (17 May 1990), 7.

Chapter 4

1. John Paul II, *Mulieris Dignitatem* (1988), #43.
2. John Paul II, *Pastores Dabo Vobis* (1992), #7.

3. John Paul II, *Sollicitudo Rei Socialis* (1987), #28.
4. *Catechism of the Catholic Church*, #876.
5. *Catechism of the Catholic Church*, #888-890.
6. Vatican II, *Lumen Gentium*, #20.
7. Vatican II, *Lumen Gentium*, #20.
8. *Catechism of the Catholic Church*, #875.
9. Tertullian, *The Prescription against the Heretics*, 21; cf. St. Clement, *First Letter to the Corinthians*, 44; and St. Irenaeus, *Against Heresies*, 3, 3.
10. The term *magisterium* comes from the Latin meaning "office of teacher."
11. Vatican II, *Dei Verbum*, #10.
12. Francis A. Sullivan, *Magisterium: Teaching Authority in the Catholic Church* (Mahwah, N.J.: Paulist Press, 1984), 29.
13. Paul VI, *Paterna cum Benevolentia* (1974), #6.
14. Vatican II, *Christus Dominus*, #13.
15. Congregation for the Doctrine of the Faith, *Instruction on the Ecclesial Vocation of the Theologian* (1990), #14.
16. Walter Kasper, *Theology and Church* (New York: Crossroad Publishing Co., 1989), 130.
17. Kasper, *Theology and Church*, 131.
18. *Catechism of the Catholic Church*, #2037.
19. Hans Urs von Balthasar, *A Short Primer for Unsettled Laymen*, tr. Michael Waldstein (San Francisco: Ignatius Press, 1985), 105.
20. Von Balthasar, *A Short Primer for Unsettled Laymen*, 110.
21. Hans Urs von Balthasar, *Unless You Become Like This Child*, tr. Erasmo Leiva (San Francisco: Ignatius Press, 1991), 53.
22. Von Balthasar, *Unless You Become Like This Child*, 53.
23. Henri de Lubac, *The Splendour of the Church*, tr. Michael Mason (New York: Paulist Press, 1963), 158.

Chapter 5

1. Walter Kasper, *Theology and Church* (New York: Crossroad Publishing Co., 1989), 130.
2. Ladislas Orsy, *The Church: Learning and Teaching* (Wilmington, Del.: Michael Glazier, Inc., 1987), 55.

3. Congregation for the Doctrine of the Faith, *Mysterium Ecclesiae* (1973), #3.
4. Vatican II, *Dei Verbum*, #11.
5. *Catechism of the Catholic Church*, #2035.
6. Vatican II, *Lumen Gentium*, #12.
7. Vatican II, *Lumen Gentium*, #12; cf. *Catechism of the Catholic Church*, #889.
8. *Catechism of the Catholic Church*, #891.
9. Vatican II, *Lumen Gentium*, #25.
10. Pope Pius IX first used the term "universal ordinary magisterium" in *Tuas Libenter* (1863). *Dei Filius*, one of the documents of Vatican I (1870), explains this way of officially teaching: "All those things are to be believed with Catholic and divine faith which are contained in the Word of God, written or handed on, and are proposed by the Church either in solemn judgment or by its ordinary and universal magisterium as divinely revealed and to be believed as such" (DS 3011).
11. Vatican II, *Lumen Gentium*, #25.
12. Vatican I, *Pastor Aeternus*, ch. 4 (DS 3071).
13. Vatican I, *Pastor Aeternus*, ch. 4 (DS 3071).
14. Vatican I, *Pastor Aeternus*, ch. 4 (DS 3074).
15. Code of Canon Law (1983), canon 749:3.
16. Vatican II, *Lumen Gentium*, #25.
17. Vatican II, *Dignitatis Humanae*, #14.
18. *Catechism of the Catholic Church*, #2036.
19. Congregation for the Doctrine of the Faith, *Instruction on the Ecclesial Vocation of the Theologian* (1990), #16.
20. *Catechism of the Catholic Church*, #892.
21. *Catechism of the Catholic Church*, #2033-2034.
22. Patrick Granfield, *The Limits of the Papacy* (New York: Crossroad Publishing Co., 1987), 158.
23. Germain Grisez, *The Way of the Lord Jesus: Christian Moral Principles*, vol. 1 (Quincy, Ill.: Franciscan Press, 1983), 851.
24. See Karl Rahner, "The Dispute concerning the Church's Teaching Office," *Theological Investigations*, vol. 14 (London: Darton, Longman & Todd, 1976), 86.

25. Vatican II, *Lumen Gentium*, #25.
26. Francis A. Sullivan, *Magisterium: Teaching Authority in the Catholic Church* (Mahwah, N.J.: Paulist Press, 1984), 164.
27. Grisez, *The Way of the Lord Jesus*, 852.

Chapter 6

1. *Spiritual Journeys*, ed. Robert Baram (Boston: Saint Paul Books & Media, 1988), 16.
2. John Paul II, *Familiaris Consortio* (1981), #6.
3. Robert N. Bellah, "Leadership Viewed from the Vantage Point of American Culture," *Origins*, 20:14 (13 September 1990), 219.
4. John Paul II, *Christifideles Laici* (1988), #40.
5. Vatican II, *Lumen Gentium*, #48; *Gaudium et Spes*, #43; *Ad Gentes*, #7, 21.
6. John Paul II, *Redemptor Hominis* (1979), #13.
7. Vatican II, *Unitatis Redintegratio*, #1.
8. Vatican II, *Lumen Gentium*, #8.
9. *Catechism of the Catholic Church*, #813.
10. Vatican II, *Unitatis Redintegratio*, #2.
11. International Theological Commission, "Select Themes on Ecclesiology on the Occasion of the Twentieth Anniversary of the Closing of the Second Vatican Council," in Michael Sharkey, ed. *International Theological Commission: Texts and Documents 1969-1985* (San Francisco: Ignatius Press, 1989), #1, 3.
12. *Catechism of the Catholic Church*, #815.
13. Vatican II, *Unitatis Redintegratio*, #1.
14. Congregation for the Doctrine of the Faith, *Mysterium Ecclesiae* (1973), #1.
15. Vatican II, *Unitatis Redintegratio*, #3.
16. Vatican II, *Lumen Gentium*, #8.
17. Vatican II, *Unitatis Redintegratio*, #3.
18. Vatican II, *Unitatis Redintegratio*, #3.
19. Vatican II, *Lumen Gentium*, #8.
20. Vatican II, *Unitatis Redintegratio*, #3.
21. Vatican II, *Unitatis Redintegratio*, #3.
22. Vatican II, *Lumen Gentium*, #14.

23. St. Cyprian of Carthage first coined this phrase: "extra Ecclesiam nulla salus" (*On the Unity of the Catholic Church*, 6).
24. *Catechism of the Catholic Church*, #846-848.
25. St. Cyprian, *Letter* 74, 7c.
26. St. Augustine, *Discourse to the People of the Church of Caesarea*, 6.
27. DS 3870.
28. Vatican II, *Lumen Gentium*, #13.
29. Vatican II, *Lumen Gentium*, #16.
30. Vatican II, *Gaudium et Spes*, #22.
31. Vatican II, *Lumen Gentium*, #14.
32. John Paul II, *Redemptoris Missio* (1990), #9, 55; see also Paul VI, *Evangelii Nuntiandi* (1975), #80.
33. Henri de Lubac, *Catholicism: Christ and the Common Destiny of Man* (San Francisco: Ignatius Press, 1988), 236. See also the 1985 statement of the International Theological Commission: "We can quite legitimately see the entire saving work of God in the world in reference to the Church, since it is in her that the means of increase in the Christ life have reached their summit and perfection" (*Select Themes on Ecclesiology*), #9, 2.
34. *Lumen Gentium*, #14, taught very clearly: "Hence they could not be saved who, knowing that the Catholic Church was founded as necessary by God through Christ, would refuse to enter it, or to remain in it."

Chapter 7

1. "Adam prefigured Christ and Adam's sleep represented the death of Christ, who had to die the sleep of death so that the Church, true mother of the living, could come from the wound in his side" (Tertullian, *The Soul*, 10.
2. *Catechism of the Catholic Church*, #796.
3. John Paul II, *Mulieris Dignitatem* (1988), #23.
4. John Paul II, *Mulieris Dignitatem* (1988), #25.
5. Vatican II, *Lumen Gentium*, #48.
6. Vatican II, *Lumen Gentium*, #64.
7. St. Zeno of Verona, *Sermons* 33, 34.

8. St. Cyprian, *Letter* 7, 74.
9. Henri de Lubac, *The Splendour of the Church*, tr. Michael Mason (New York: Paulist Press, 1963), 145.
10. Vatican II made frequent references to the holiness of the Church: It was God's will to "call together all those who believe in Christ to form a holy Church" (*Lumen Gentium*, #2); "the mystery of holy Church is manifested in her foundation" (*Lumen Gentium*, #5); cf. *Lumen Gentium*, #8, 10, 12, 48.
11. *Catechism of the Catholic Church*, #823.
12. Vatican II, *Lumen Gentium*, #9.
13. *Catechism of the Catholic Church*, #827.
14. Vatican II, *Lumen Gentium*, #8.
15. Vatican II, *Lumen Gentium*, #15.
16. Vatican I, *Dei Filius*, ch. 3 (DS 3013).
17. *Catechism of the Catholic Church*, #828.
18. Hans Urs von Balthasar, *Elucidations*, tr. John Riches (London: S.P.C.K., 1975), 214.

Chapter 8

1. *Catechism of the Catholic Church*, #463.
2. *Catechism of the Catholic Church*, #461-469.
3. Christopher Derrick, *Sex and Sacredness* (San Francisco: Ignatius Press, 1982), 73.
4. John Paul II, *The Original Unity of Man and Woman* (Boston: Saint Paul Books & Media, 1981), 175.
5. *Catechism of the Catholic Church*, #1147.
6. St. Augustine, *Sermon* 191.
7. Godfried Danneels, "Christ or Aquarius," *Catholic International* 2:10 (15-31 May 1991), 487.
8. Louis Bouyer, *Cosmos: The World and the Glory of God* (Petersham, Mass.: St. Bede's Publications, 1988), 98.
9. Henri de Lubac, *A Brief Catechesis on Nature and Grace*, tr. Richard Arnandez (San Francisco: Ignatius Press, 1984), 213.
10. Thomas Howard, *Evangelical Is Not Enough* (San Francisco: Ignatius Press, 1984), 29.
11. Vatican II, *Sacrosanctum Concilium*, #5.

12. Vatican II, *Lumen Gentium*, #8.
13. *Catechism of the Catholic Church*, #1076.
14. Leo the Great, *Sermon* 74, 2. See also St. Ambrose: "Thou hast shown thyself to me face to face, O Christ; I find thee in thy sacraments" (PL 14, 975).
15. Daniel Callam, "An Old Answer to a New Question," *Canadian Catholic Review* 10:9 (October, 1992), 2-3.
16. St. Augustine, *Homilies on the Gospel of John*, 5, 18. See also the teaching of St. Thomas: "The ministers of the Church can confer the sacraments even when they are evil" (*Summa Theologiae*, III, q. 64, a. 5c).
17. See John Paul II's writings collected by the Daughters of St. Paul in *The Original Unity of Man and Woman* (1981); *Blessed Are the Pure of Heart: Analysis of Chastity for Single or Married* (1983); *Reflections on "Humanae Vitae"* (1984); and *The Theology of Marriage and Celibacy* (1986). All are published by Saint Paul Books & Media of Boston.
18. Laurence F. X. Brett, *Redeemed Creation: The Sacramentals Today* (Wilmington, Del.: Michael Glazier, Inc., 1984), 12.
19. Vatican II, *Sacrosanctum Concilium*, #61.
20. Louis Bouyer, *Rite and Man* (Notre Dame: University of Notre Dame Press, 1963), 67.
21. Peter Kreeft, *Fundamentals of the Faith: Essays in Christian Apologetics* (San Francisco: Ignatius Press, 1988), 284.

Chapter 9

1. Vatican II, *Lumen Gentium*, #11; cf. *Presbyterorum Ordinis*, #5, and *Catechism of the Catholic Church*, #1324-1327.
2. St. Thomas Aquinas, *Summa Theologiae*, III, q. 83, a. 4.
3. Peter Kreeft, *Fundamentals of the Faith: Essays in Christian Apologetics* (San Francisco: Ignatius Press, 1988), 286.
4. Hans Urs von Balthasar, *The Von Balthasar Reader*, ed. Medard Kehl and Werner Loser (New York: Crossroad Publishing Co., 1982), 283.
5. Von Balthasar, *Elucidations*, tr. John Riches (London: S.P.C.K., 1975), 120.

6. Von Balthasar, *You Crown the Year with Your Goodness: Sermons Through the Liturgical Year*, tr. Graham Harrison (San Francisco: Ignatius Press, 1989), 147.
7. John Paul II, *Mulieris Dignitatem* (1988), #26.
8. *Catechism of the Catholic Church,* #1362-1372.
9. Vatican II, *Sacrosanctum Concilium*, #47.
10. *Catechism of the Catholic Church*, #1374-1377.
11. St. Cyril of Alexandria, *Catechetical Lectures*, 19.
12. DS 700.
13. DS 802.
14. DS 1636; cf. DS 1652; Paul VI, *Mysterium Fidei* (1965), #46.
15. Paul VI, *Mysterium Fidei* (1965), #55.
16. Kreeft, *Fundamentals of the Faith*, 282.
17. St. Thomas Aquinas, *Summa Theologiae*, III, q. 66, a. 6.
18. John Paul II, *Redemptor Hominis* (1979), #20.
19. Jean Galot, *The Eucharistic Heart* (San Francisco: Ignatius Press, 1990), 122.
20. *Catechism of the Catholic Church*, #1392.
21. Von Balthasar, *You Crown the Year with Your Goodness*, 149.
22. DS 1638; cf. *Catechism of the Catholic Church*, #1394-1395.
23. St. Augustine, *Sermon* 272.
24. *Catechism of the Catholic Church*, #1396.
25. John Paul II, *Dominicae Cenae* (1980), #4.
26. Joseph Ratzinger, *Feast of Faith*, tr. Graham Harrison (San Francisco: Ignatius Press, 1986), 84.
27. Vatican II, *Gaudium et Spes*, #43.
28. John Paul II, "Eucharist: Apex of Christian Life," *The Pope Speaks*, 37:5 (1992), 350.
29. John Paul II, *Sollicitudo Rei Socialis* (1987), #48.
30. John Paul II, *Dominicae Cenae* (1980), #6.
31. Walter Kasper, *Theology and Church* (New York: Crossroad Publishing Co., 1989), 191; cf. *Catechism of the Catholic Church*, #1397.
32. James Quinn, *The Theology of the Eucharist* (Hales Corners, Wisc.: Clergy Book Service, 1973), 89.
33. DS 1638.

34. Von Balthasar, *Elucidations*, 212.
35. Kreeft, *Fundamentals of the Faith*, 286.

Chapter 10

1. Thomas Howard, *Chance or the Dance? A Critique of Modern Secularism* (San Francisco: Ignatius Press, 1989), 110.
2. *Catechism of the Catholic Church*, #2332.
3. *Catechism of the Catholic Church*, #356-361.
4. *Catechism of the Catholic Church*, #1701-1705.
5. Peter Brown, *The Body and Society: Men, Women and Sexual Renunciation in Early Christianity* (New York: Columbia University Press, 1990), 26.
6. John Paul II, *The Original Unity of Man and Woman* (Boston: Saint Paul Books & Media, 1981), 109.
7. John Paul II, *The Original Unity of Man and Woman*, 107.
8. John Paul II, *The Original Unity of Man and Woman*, 114.
9. John Paul II, *The Original Unity of Man and Woman*, 371-372.
10. John Paul II, *The Original Unity of Man and Woman*, 144.
11. Paul Quay, *Christian Meaning of Human Sexuality* (San Francisco: Ignatius Press, 1988), 36.
12. *Catechism of the Catholic Church*, #400.
13. John Paul II, *Blessed Are the Pure of Heart: Analysis of Chastity for Single or Married* (Boston: Saint Paul Books & Media, 1988), 75.
14. John Paul II, *The Original Unity of Man and Woman*, 143.
15. John Paul II, *The Theology of Marriage and Celibacy* (Boston: Saint Paul Books & Media, 1986), 333.
16. John Paul II, *Blessed Are the Pure of Heart*, 244.
17. John Paul II, *Blessed Are the Pure of Heart*, 258.
18. Peter Kreeft, *Making Choices* (Ann Arbor, Mich.: Servant Publications, 1990), 101.
19. *Catechism of the Catholic Church*, #2354.
20. John Paul II, *Familiaris Consortio* (1981), #80.
21. John Paul II, *Familiaris Consortio* (1981), #80.
22. *Blessed Are the Pure of Heart*, 110; cf. *Catechism of the Catholic Church*, #2380-2381.

23. *Catechism of the Catholic Church*, #1644-1651, 2382-2386.
24. *Catechism of the Catholic Church*, #2366-2372.
25. John Paul II, *Mulieris Dignitatem* (1988), #18.
26. Quay, *Christian Meaning of Human Sexuality*, 35.
27. Paul VI, *Humanae Vitae* (1968), #12.
28. John Paul II, *Reflections on "Humanae Vitae"* (Boston: Saint Paul Books & Media, 1984), 10.
29. John Paul II, *Familiaris Consortio* (1981), #32.
30. John Paul II, *Familiaris Consortio* (1981), #32.

Chapter 11

1. John Paul, *Redemptoris Missio* (1990), #11.
2. Congregation for the Doctrine of the Faith, *Libertatis Conscientia* (1986), #63.
3. American Bishops, *To the Ends of the Earth: A Pastoral Statement on World Mission 1987* (Washington, D.C.: U.S. Catholic Conference, 1987), #31.
4. 1971 Synod of Bishops, *Justice in the World*, #6.
5. Vatican II, *Gaudium et Spes*, #69.
6. John Paul II, *Centesimus Annus* (1991), #31; cf. *Laborem Exercens* (1981), #14, and *Catechism of the Catholic Church*, #2402.
7. *Catechism of the Catholic Church*, #2419-2422.
8. John Paul II, *Centesimus Annus* (1991), #5.
9. John Paul II, *Ex Corde Ecclesiae* (1990), #33.
10. Vatican II, *Gaudium et Spes*, #76; cf. John Paul II, *Centesimus Annus* (1991), #55.
11. John Paul, *Redemptor Hominis* (1979), #13; cf. *Catechism of the Catholic Church*, #356-360.
12. Vatican II, *Gaudium et Spes*, #22.
13. John Paul II, *Redemptor Hominis* (1979), #13.
14. John Paul II, *Christifideles Laici* (1988), #37.
15. John Paul II, *Christifideles Laici* (1988), #37.
16. *Catechism of the Catholic Church*, #1930-1933.
17. John Paul II, *Christifideles Laici* (1988), #38.
18. American Bishops, "A Century of Social Teaching: A Common

Heritage, A Continuing Challenge," *Origins*, 20:24 (22 November 1990), 395.
19. John Paul II, *Pastores Dabo Vobis* (1992), #7.
20. *Catechism of the Catholic Church*, #1905-1912.
21. John Paul II, *Sollicitudo Rei Socialis* (1987), #38.
22. John Paul II, *Sollicitudo Rei Socialis* (1987), #40.
23. John Paul II, *Redemptoris Missio* (1990), #60; cf. *Catechism of the Catholic Church*, #2448.
24. American Bishops, *Economic Justice for All: Pastoral Letter in Catholic Social Teaching and U.S. Economy* (Washington, D.C.: U.S. Catholic Conference, 1986), #24.
25. John Paul II, *Centesimus Annus* (1991), #48; cf. *Catechism of the Catholic Church*, #1883-1885.
26. *Catechism of the Catholic Church*, #2207.
27. John Paul II, *Familiaris Consortio* (1981), #86; cf. John Paul II, *Christifideles Laici* (1988), #40.
28. John Paul II, *Familiaris Consortio* (1981), #64.
29. John Paul II, *Centesimus Annus* (1991), #39.
30. John Paul II, *Familiaris Consortio* (1981), #43.
31. John Paul II, *Familiaris Consortio* (1981), #45; cf. Leo XIII, *Rerum Novarum* (1891), #12.
32. Vatican II, *Lumen Gentium*, #31.
33. John Paul II, *Christifideles Laici* (1988), #17.
34. Vatican II, *Lumen Gentium*, #36.
35. John Paul II, *Christifideles Laici* (1988), #42.
36. John Paul II, *Centesimus Annus* (1991), #5.

Chapter 12

1. Avery Dulles, "Towards a Renewed Papacy," in *The Resilient Church* (New York: Doubleday & Co., Inc., 1977), 113.
2. *Catechism of the Catholic Church*, #880-882.
3. John Paul II, "Christ Builds His Church on Peter," *L'Osservatore Romano*, 48 (2 December 1992), 19.
4. St. Leo the Great, *Sermon* 3.
5. Joseph Ratzinger, "The Primacy of Peter," *L'Osservatore Romano*, 27 (8 July 1991), 7.

6. John Paul II, "Peter Strengthens His Brothers in Faith," *L'Osservatore Romano*, 49 (9 December 1992), 15.
7. John Paul II, "Peter Charged with Feeding the Sheep," *L'Osservatore Romano*, 50 (16 December 1992), 11.
8. John Paul II, "Peter Allows Gentiles To Be Baptized," *L'Osservatore Romano*, 3 (20 January 1993), 11.
9. John Paul II, "Peter Ranks First among the Apostles," *L'Osservatore Romano*, 51/52 (23/30 December 1992), 9.
10. St. Clement, *First Letter to the Corinthians*, 5-6.
11. St. Irenaeus, *Against Heresies*, 3, 3.
12. St. Jerome, *Letter to Pope Damasus*, 15, 2.
13. Paul VI, *Insegnamenti di Paolo VI*, vol. 4 (Vatican City: Polyglot Press, 1967), 1013.
14. Pedro Rodriguez, "The Primacy of the Pope in the Church," in *On Being Catholics*, ed. Charles Connolly (Houston: Lumen Christi Press, 1983), 60.
15. New Zealand Bishops, "In the Service of Church Unity," *L'Osservatore Romano*, 32/33 (12/19 August 1991), 6-7.
16. Vatican I, *Pastor Aeternus*, intro., DS 3051; cf. Vatican II, *Lumen Gentium*, #18.
17. Paul VI, *Paterna cum Benevolentia* (1974), #2.
18. New Zealand Bishops, "In the Service of Church Unity," *L'Osservatore Romano*, 7.
19. Vatican I, *Pastor Aeternus*, ch. 3, DS 3064.
20. Vatican I, *Pastor Aeternus*, ch. 3, DS 3061.
21. Vatican I, *Pastor Aeternus*, ch. 3, DS 3062.
22. Vatican I, *Pastor Aeternus*, ch. 3, DS 3064.
23. Vatican I, *Pastor Aeternus*, ch. 3, DS 3060.
24. Vatican I, *Pastor Aeternus*, intro., DS 3052.
25. Vatican I, *Pastor Aeternus*, ch. 3, DS 3059.

A Concluding Checklist

1. Henri de Lubac, *The Splendour of the Church*, tr. Michael Mason (New York: Paulist Press, 1963), 145.

Enriching new booklets that fill your spiritual needs

Sharing Your Faith:
A User's Guide to Evangelization
By Bert Ghezzi
No. 169, $1.50.

What We Believe About the Saints
By J. Michael Miller, C.S.B.
No. 170, $1.50.

Forgiveness
By Archbishop Daniel E. Pilarczyk
No. 171, $1.50.

Mary in the Bible: Questions and Answers
By Rev. John H. Hampsch, C.M.F.
No. 174, $1.50.

Father Roberts' Guide to Personal Prayer
By Father Kenneth Roberts
No. 176, $1.50.

A Catholic Understanding of the Gospels
By Peter M.J. Stravinskas
No. 175, $1.50.

Available at bookstores. Credit card holders may order direct from Our Sunday Visitor by calling toll-free 1-800-348-2440. Or, send payment plus $3.95 shipping/handling to: Our Sunday Visitor / 200 Noll Plaza / Huntington, IN 46750.

Prices and availability subject to change.

OUR SUNDAY VISITOR BOOKS